THE FOUNDATION STONE

THE FOUNDATION STONE

Willem Zeylmans van Emmichoven

TEMPLE LODGE

Translated from German by John Davy

Temple Lodge Publishing
Hillside House, The Square
Forest Row, East Sussex
RH18 5ES

www.templelodge.com

Reprinted by Temple Lodge 2002
First published in English translation by Rudolf Steiner Press 1963

Originally published in German under the title *Der Grundstein* by Verlag Freies Geistesleben, Stuttgart, 1956

A catalogue record for this book is available from the British Library

ISBN 1 902636 37 6

Cover by Andrew Morgan

Printed and bound in Great Britain by 4edge Limited, Essex

Contents

TRANSLATOR'S NOTE

A number of words and phrases of the Foundation Stone Meditation are woven into the text by the author from time to time. Where this occurs, the corresponding English words or phrases of the revised translation by George Adams have been used, even if they occasionally seem to fit awkwardly into the rest of the sentence. (The revised translation is published in *The Foundation Stone*, London 1996.)

THE FOUNDATION STONE

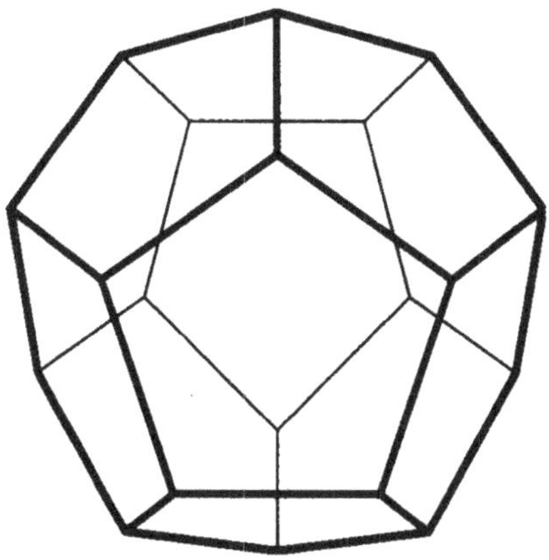

Menschenseele!
Du lebest in den Gliedern,
Die dich durch die Raumeswelt
In das Geistesmeereswesen tragen:
Übe *Geist-Erinnern*
In Seelentiefen,
Wo in waltendem
Weltenschöpfer-Sein
Das eigne Ich
Im Gottes-Ich
Erweset;
Und du wirst wahrhaft *leben*
Im Menschen-Welten-Wesen.

Denn es waltet der Vater-Geist der Höhen
In den Weltentiefen Sein-erzeugend:
Ihr Kräfte-Geister
Lasset aus den Höhen erklingen,
Was in den Tiefen das Echo findet;
Dieses spricht:
Aus dem Göttlichen weset die Menschheit.
Das hören die Geister in Ost, West, Nord, Süd:
Menschen mögen es hören.

Menschenseele!
Du lebest in dem Herzens-Lungen-Schlage,
Der dich durch den Zeitenrhythmus
In's eigne Seelenwesensfuhlen leitet:
Übe *Geist-Besinnen*
Im Seelengleichgewichte,
Wo die wogenden

Soul of Man!
Thou livest in the Limbs
Which bear thee through the world of Space
Into the ocean-being of the Spirit.
Practise *Spirit-recollection*
In depths of soul,
Where in the wielding
World-Creator-Life
Thine own I
Comes to being
Within the I of God.
Then in the All-World-Being of Man
Thou wilt truly *live.*

For the Father-Spirit of the Heights holds sway
In Depths of Worlds begetting Life.
Spirits of Strength!
Let this ring out from the Heights
And in the Depths be echoed,
Speaking:
From God, Mankind has Being.
The Spirits hear it in East and West and North and South:
May human beings hear it!

Soul of Man!
Thou livest in the beat of Heart and Lung
Which leads thee through the rhythmic tides of Time
Into the feeling of thine own Soul-being.
Practise *Spirit-mindfulness*
In balance of the soul,
Where the surging

Welten-Werde-Taten
Das eigne Ich
Dem Welten-Ich
Vereinen;
Und du wirst wahrhaft fühlen
Im Menschen-Seelen-Wirken.

Denn es waltet der Christus-Wille im Umkreis
In den Weltenrhythmen Seelen-begnadend;
Ihr Lichtes-Geister
Lasset vom Osten befeuern,
Was durch den Westen sich formet;
Dieses spricht:
In dem Christus wird Leben der Tod.
Das hören die Geister in Ost, West, Nord, Süd:
Menschen mögen es hören.

Menschenseele!
Du lebest im ruhenden Haupte,
Das dir aus Ewigkeitsgründen
Die Weltgedanken erschliesset:
Übe *Geist-Erschauen*
In Gedanken-Ruhe,
Wo die ew'gen Götterziele
Welten-Wesens-Licht
Dem eignen Ich
Zu freiem Wollen
Schenken;
Und du wirst wahrhaft *denken*
In Menschen-Geistes-Gründen.

Deeds of the World's Becoming
Do thine own I
Unite
Unto the I of the World.
Then 'mid the weaving of the Soul of Man
Thou wilt truly *feel*.

For the Christ-Will in the encircling Round holds sway
In the Rhythms of the Worlds, blessing the Soul.
Spirits of Light!
Let this be fired from the East
And through the West be formèd,
Speaking:
In Christ, Death becomes Life.
The Spirits hear it in East and West and North and South:
May humans beings hear it!

Soul of Man!
Thou livest in the resting Head
Which from the ground of the Eternal
Opens to thee the Thoughts of Worlds.
Practise *Spirit-vision*
In quietness of Thought,
Where the eternal aims of Gods
World-Being's Light
On thine own I
Bestow
For thy free Willing.
Then from the ground of the Spirit in Man
Thou wilt truly *think*.

Denn es walten des Geistes Weltgedanken
Im Weltenwesen Licht-erflehend;
Ihr Seelen-Geister
Lasset aus den Tiefen erbitten,
Was in den Höhen erhöret wird;
Dieses spricht:
In des Geistes Weltgedanken erwachet die Seele.
Das hören die Geister in Ost, West, Nord, Süd:
Menschen mögen es hören.

In der Zeiten Wende
Trat das Welten-Geistes-Licht
In den irdischen Wesensstrom;
Nacht-Dunkel
Hatte ausgewaltet;
Taghelles Licht
Erstrahlte in Menschenseelen;
Licht,
Das erwärmet
Die armen Hirtenherzen;
Licht,
Das erleuchtet
Die weisen Königshäupter.

For the Spirit's Universal Thoughts hold sway
In the Beings of all Worlds, craving for Light.
Spirits of Soul!
Let this be prayed in the Depths
And from the Heights be answered,
Speaking:
In the Spirit's Universal Thoughts, the Soul awakens.
The Spirits hear it in East and West and North and
May human beings hear it! South:

At the turning-point of Time
The Spirit-Light of the World
Entered the stream of Earthly Being.
Darkness of Night
Had held its sway;
Day-radiant Light
Poured in the souls of men;
Light that gives Warmth
To simple Shepherds' Hearts,
Light that enlightens
The wise Head of Kings.

Göttliches Licht,
Christus-Sonne,
Erwärme
Unsere Herzen,
Erleuchte
Unsere Häupter,—
Dass gut werde,
Was wir
Aus Herzen gründen,
Was wir
Aus Häuptern
Zielvoll führen
Wollen.

(Text of the Foundation Stone Meditation as given by Rudolf Steiner to the members of the General Anthroposophical Society, published in the *Nachrichtenblatt*, Number 1, 13th January, 1924.)

O Light Divine,
O Sun of Christ!
Warm Thou
Our Hearts,
Enlighten Thou
Our Heads,
That good may become
What from our Hearts we would found
And from our Heads direct
With single purpose.

(Revised translation by George Adams, assisted by Dr. Maria Roeschl-Lehrs, Miss E. Hersey, Dr. E. Lehrs and Dr. Heidenreich, first published in 1942, and included in *The Foundation Stone*, London 1957).

Introduction

When the Foundation Stone of the General Anthroposophical Society was laid, it was possible to experience the event as a Mystery, whose deep significance will only reveal itself to mankind as time goes on. Rudolf Steiner said at the time that his task was to give to the Society the form "needed to foster the Anthroposophical Movement". A few months later, at Arnhem, he spoke of the re-founding, the "actual foundation of the General Anthroposophical Society."*

It is not possible to assess the Christmas Meeting of 1923 properly if it is seen as something which is important only for the circle of members. The meaning of this Mystery—the laying of the Foundation Stone—is much more far-reaching. In this book an attempt will be made to indicate something of its significance.

Some things it will only be possible to hint at. The most important matters cannot be expressed concretely at all, since they concern a process which is still going on and can only reveal itself fully in the distant future. Nevertheless, some picture of this future may perhaps emerge from between the lines.

The laying of the Foundation Stone in 1923 was not an isolated event: it was a deed which is best considered

*Lecture given at Arnhem, 18th July, 1924.

in conjunction with a series of events. To begin with, there was the laying of the Foundation Stone for the first Goetheanum in September 1913. Then came the construction of the building itself, and finally the fire which destroyed it before it was complete. A year later came the laying of the Foundation Stone for the General Anthroposophical Society and the High School for Spiritual Science. Nine months later, Rudolf Steiner fell ill, and left the physical world after six months' illness.

Today mankind is standing at the threshold of the spiritual world. The period from the first Foundation Stone to Rudolf Steiner's death, if viewed as a whole, appears as a kind of spiritual attempt to prepare a group of people for higher future tasks by means of an initiation. This initiation proceeded by the stages described above. Its peculiarity was that it took in ever larger groups of people, and addressed them with increasing directness as a community born out of the spirit. Naturally, the initiation meant here had been prepared in the case of many individuals for years previously. The entire life-work of Rudolf Steiner, beginning in the eighties of the last century, was devoted to this task.*

The foundations were laid for the way of initiation proper to this age. To begin with, each person must tread this path on his own. But its essential feature is that the pupil, as he learns to know himself more deeply as an individual, begins also to experience himself as a part of

*It should be unnecessary to emphasise that this series of events can be interpreted in various ways. The author felt it to be his duty to treat them from his own point of view.

humanity as a whole. The Ego of each individual is prepared to become the bearer of the Ego of mankind. The individual human being grows towards humanity; mankind lives as a whole in each individual.

The 1913 Foundation Stone

The laying of the foundation stone for the "Johannesbau" ("St. John's Building")—as it was then still called—took place in Dornach on 20th September, 1913. A report of this event exists from which it is clear that this act was woven into the fabric of both the spiritual and the physical worlds. Rudolf Steiner first turned to the four points of the compass in succession and then called upon the higher Hierarchies to protect and guide the deed which was being performed. As is well known, the Foundation Stone was a double pentagonal dodecahedron, which was shaped "as an emblem of the human soul". "Its doubly twelve-membered form" said Rudolf Steiner, "represents for us an emblem of the striving human soul immersed as a microcosm in the macrocosm." Later he repeated that this stone "is formed according to the cosmic images of the human soul", or, as he also expressed it, "formed as the corner-stone of the human being who desires to seek for himself in the spirit, to feel himself in the world's soul, to divine himself in the world's Ego".

It is thus clear that the proposed Goetheanum, connected as it was in the closest possible way with this Foundation Stone, was to become a unified being, and in it were to live the same cosmic forces which form the human soul. A tremendous sense of responsibility towards the whole being and evolution of the earth emerges from the address which Rudolf Steiner gave on this occasion. He said that the Goetheanum would be a "visible sign" of the spiritual life of the new age. This spiritual life he characterised as a great mission of mankind on the planet earth. The powers of darkness would grow steadily stronger; because of them the souls of mankind today would grow parched and barren; the spiritual battle which has to be waged is directed primarily against these spirits of darkness.*

It is hardly possible to comment on this address. The overwhelming words uttered by Dr. Steiner can be read. Here it is enough to point out that on this occasion, for the first time, something of the content of the Fifth Gospel was expressed. This, Steiner said, was to sound "from out of the West as the oldest Gospel", and "the Macrocosmic Gospel shall sound forth like an echo towards the Gospel of the East".

Just as the four Gospels went out from the East and worked towards the West, so there now comes from out of the West the "Gospel of Knowledge". As the principal content of this Fifth Gospel, Rudolf Steiner then gave the Macrocosmic Lord's Prayer, a "macrocosmic world prayer, which is connected with the Moon and with Jupiter, as the four Gospels are connected with the Earth".

AUM, Amen!
Es walten die Übel,
Zeugen sich lösender Ichheit,

**Aus den Inhalten der esoterischen Schule, Heft II,* Dornach 1948. English translation: *From the Contents of the Esoteric School, Volume II* London, 1949.

Von andern erschuldete Selbstheitschuld,
Erlebet im täglichen Brote,
In dem nicht waltet der Himmel Wille,
Da der Mensch sich schied von Eurem Reich
Und vergass Euren Namen,
Ihr Väter in den Himmeln.

AUM, Amen!
The Evils hold sway,
Witness of Egoity becoming free,
Selfhood-Guilt through others incurred,
Experienced in the Daily Bread,
Wherein the Will of the Heavens does not rule,
In that Man severed himself from Your Kingdom,
And forgot Your Names,
Ye Fathers in the Heavens.*

Whoever allows this Macrocosmic Lord's Prayer to speak within him during meditation, experiences most deeply the pain of the incarnation which the whole of mankind has undergone since the Lemurian age. From out of this suffering, Christ could give to His Apostles the Lord's Prayer as a redeeming world-prayer. Out of a knowledge of the divine powers which lead into the depths of the earthly forces, Rudolf Steiner could perform deeds on earth which brought the true Christ Mystery nearer to man in an age which demands that each person should experience such knowledge individually.

**Aus der Akasha-Forschung. Das fünfte Evangelium*, im Selbstverlag, herausgegeben Marie Steiner, Dornach 1948 and 1955. English translation, *The Fifth Gospel*, London, 1978.

During the next ten years, the Goetheanum grew up like a spiritual plant from the seed of the Foundation Stone. When one saw it in spring, among the blossoming fruit trees, it became especially clear that it was no ordinary building. One realised that it was a Being, formed out of living forces—out of etheric forces, in fact.

The double dodecahedron of the Foundation Stone was laid so that the larger part was directed towards the East, where the smaller dome rose, while the smaller part faced West, in the direction of the larger dome. Inside the earth, the cosmic and earthly laws are expressed in mineral form; above the earth the Goetheanum rose, an expression of etheric laws. This was apparent in the way the rigid forms of the Foundation Stone reappeared in the Goetheanum building in manifold variations and metamorphoses of the original *ur*-form. How could it be otherwise? For Rudolf Steiner said that the building was to be a place in which the soul of man could find the spirit. He also said that the Goetheanum and the content of Anthroposophy formed an inward unity—they were related as a nut is to its shell. The forms corresponded—in fact he once compared the forms of the Goetheanum with the cake-mould in which a pound-cake (*Napfkuchen*) is baked. He gave a precise description of these relationships when he spoke about the spiritual formative forces.

He said that these were forces "which live in the spirit, and have the power to impress themselves on that which surrounds us as a sheath in our building".

On another occasion he said that the building was a living word, an organ of speech for the spirit, a signpost to the spirit. He summed up the Goetheanum when he called it a "House of Speech" ("*Haus der Sprache*").* This House of Speech was visible on earth. Now that it has been destroyed by fire, it can be found in the spiritual world as an Imagination. It is, in fact, a task of modern humanity to concern itself inwardly with it in Imagination.

How may one learn to understand this mysterious building and its meaning for modern man?

The double dome of the building rested on a concrete foundation. The form of this foundation was fitted to the bed rock. In the outline of the building there appeared two interpenetrating circles, related in a way which expresses the present stage of development of man. The spiritual world, and the consciousness which has been developed in the physical world, are in contact with each other, but interpenetrate only partially, and present in their mutual relationship a problem with which modern humanity has to struggle.

On this foundation, the two domed halls rose, made of wood. The larger dome was borne on two sets of seven pillars; the smaller, on twelve pillars. The whole had only one axis of symmetry, running from the western entrance eastwards. A person who entered the building

* *Wege zu einem neuen Baustil*, *Stuttgart* 1982. English translation, *Ways to a new style in Architecture*, Rudolf Steiner Press, London, 1984.

and walked east, passed a row of pillars whose forms displayed a constant metamorphosis. He could experience in his soul a parallel development and metamorphosis, leading from Old Saturn to the Venus condition of our earth. Dr. Steiner said that this was the Will-axis, the direction of the Will.*

When the soul expands upward with the vertical growth of the pillars, it can experience the impulses of Feeling. These are eventually completed high up in the forms of the dome, and lead to the impulses of Thinking. From out of the dome, the secrets of the spiritual development of the whole of mankind work in coloured surfaces. When a person experiences this inwardly, the etheric forces in the region of his head detach themselves slightly, and the profound inner significance of the paintings on the dome becomes apparent. Thus it is possible to experience how the human soul can relate itself to the forms of the Goetheanum, and to the building as a whole, in thinking, feeling and willing.

The architectural impulse which was given here was something quite new for the evolution of the earth. The really great buildings of mankind, of course, have always sprung from a clear spiritual understanding of the state of consciousness of the age in question; thus the great Indian temples grew up out of the earth like spiritualised nature-forces; the Egyptian buildings expressed an awareness of mortality; the harmonious forms of the Greek

**Der Dornacher Bau als Wahrzeichen geschichtlichen Werdens und künstlerischer Umwandlungsimpulse*, Dornach 1937. Typescript translation R.-LX1 available to members of the Anthroposophical Society.

temples were likewise related to the age. But for our time Dr. Steiner was concerned to create a building which was not only to serve an external purpose, but which would correspond in a new way to the inner needs of mankind—and at the same time express in a quite concrete way the spiritual content of these needs. Thus the Goetheanum helped the spiritual development of our age by demonstrating directly to humanity a path from the physical sense world into the worlds of Imagination and Inspiration.

If one entered the Goetheanum without making aesthetic judgements in the usual way, giving oneself up to it completely, waiting for it, for this Being, to accept one—then one could come to a new experience of space. Architectural spaces are usually closed in some way—but in the Goetheanum the opposite was the case; the soul was not confined by the walls, did not bump up against them, so to speak. Instead a feeling emerged of being led further into the world of the spirit through the forms which were made visible there. The forms of the wall were alive and embraced the forces of the soul, so that they could expand and unite themselves with the cosmos.

These living forms could arise because they were derived from the same etheric laws which govern the growth of plants. They were organs through which spirituality could be directly expressed. Rudolf Steiner said, with reason, that such forms could become larynges, which the Gods could use in order to speak to us.

The walls were not only formed in a living way, but were also partly transparent. The glass windows, in their various colours, were ground so that forms were created by the light streaming in from outside. "This whole relief structure is an organ for the speech of the gods, that they may speak to us from all quarters of the universe." From them sounded forth the words: "Thus dost thou find, oh Man, the way to the Spirit". The glass etchings revealed to us a path of initiation, different aspects of which appeared on each side.*

In the purely architectural forms, the laws of the surrounding external world were expressed—for instance, in the remarkable load-bearing forms of the stairs leading from the lower part of the building upwards. Similarly, etheric-physical forms were made visible in the rich modelling of the wood, while in the windows and paintings the colours were drawn from the realm of the etheric.

The way in which the colours were applied—especially in the smaller dome—was also quite new. The figures emerged from out of the colours. This was a colour language which modern painters like Kandinsky and others had been seeking for years. The colours, although not always superficially perfect, revealed their inner nature in a remarkable way. For example, the Faust-like figure, which strives towards the fully conscious Ego, is born entirely out of mysterious, mystical blue; a child flies towards it, painted in orange; a dark, black skeleton with a book under its arm stands adjacent. Above floats the Inspiring Angel, again in delicate blue. It is impossible

**Rudolf Steiner's Entwürfe für die Glasfenster des Goetheanum*, Dornach 1961. Previous edition *Die Goetheanum Fenster-Motive*, Dornach 1935; English translation *The Goetheanum Windows* London and New York, 1938.

simply to study the meaning of these paintings in a theoretical way; instead, the soul itself is changed and inwardly influenced by the forces of the colours.

The foregoing has shown how a physical space was transformed into an etheric one. In the same way, *time* could be experienced, in the Goetheanum, as an interplay of the forces of life and death. In the colours there is already a transition to that which expresses itself musically in the rhythms of time. Used as described above, these colours acted as a bridge to what Pythagoras still experienced as the music of the spheres. But an immediate experience of time could be had in connection with the intervals between the motives of the pillars. Here the most important thing was not so much the immediate forms themselves as that which worked across from one capital to the next. If one considered the simple form of the so-called Saturn pillar, in which the upper and the lower parts met in a clearcut way, and then passed on to the motives of the Sun pillar, and saw there the first metamorphosis of these simple forms, one could feel how in the passage between the two an inner development of consciousness had taken place. But in the interval, the first forms had to die in order to be born again on a new level. In such dying and growing a new experience of time could be had.

The total effect of the rounded heavenly forms of the domes was of an eternity coming to completion between space and time. It had been planned that the Christ statue would stand at the end of this aisle, against the eastern wall of the small dome—Christ, the Representative of Mankind, stepping forward and holding the balance between the forces of Lucifer and Ahriman. Rudolf Steiner, who carved the main parts of the statue himself, once said how difficult it was to express all this in plastic forms. "The entire robe", he said, "should be pouring out love".

Looking at the face, the lines of the forehead in strong relief gave the impression that here was the confluence of all the wisdom of the world. Wisdom and love, meeting in the breast, gave direction and meaning to the two arms, which directed Lucifer and Ahriman upwards and downwards into their spheres of activity in world-evolution.

In the Goetheanum, therefore, the human soul found itself living in etheric space, awakening and dying in great rhythms of time, feeling itself contained in the eternal being of the Creation; and finally encountering the Being of the Ego of mankind, perceiving the Resurrection.

When, after ten years, the still unfinished Goetheanum was destroyed by fire, it meant more than grief at the destruction of a building on which many people had worked with great devotion under the personal guidance of Rudolf Steiner. Rather it was as if a living spiritual being had been taken from mankind. A friend asked Rudolf Steiner about the deepest reason for his grief. He is said to have replied that it was not merely the loss of the Goetheanum, but the fact that so many human beings in the West would no longer be able to contemplate these forms. This reply can be well understood. It is the western world, enmeshed in powers of thought formed according to the sense-world, which has to struggle hardest with materialism. Simply looking at the forms of the Goetheanum could have led many people's powers of thought towards Imagination, even if only unconsciously.

A year later, Rudolf Steiner was able to make a new design for the second Goetheanum. He emphasised this did not mean that the form of the original Goetheanum could be repeated. The second building was to be more a castle, a fortification, less vulnerable and delicate than the first, built entirely of concrete. Of course, important metamorphoses of the forms of the first Goetheanum are to be recognised in the second. Nevertheless, it must be stressed that the whole being of the first was unique. In the imaginative language of its forms and colours it was a complete representation of Anthroposophy, as it could be brought down to earth from the spiritual world; and human souls, who were descended from out of the same spiritual realms, could feel at home there as though in their proper spiritual environment. They found the primal spiritual image of their own being made visible around them. Anthroposophia lived in this building in visible form.

The Fire

The Goetheanum went up in flames during the New Year's night of 1922/23. This was not simply the consequence of the attack of an enemy. It also expressed a failure of the members of the Anthroposophical Society. Rudolf Steiner pointed to this plainly. In his opening address to the Christmas Foundation Meeting, he said that the heap of ruins on the Dornach hill was in certain respects a symbol of other heaps of ruins inside the Anthroposophical Society, and of conditions in the world generally.*

Since 1902, the Society—in which Rudolf Steiner had been elected Secretary of the German section of the Theosophical Society—had gone through various phases. These were sketched in the address quoted above. In the first phase, which comprised about seven years, the life of the Society was carried on apart from the outside world. The members were mostly gathered into small groups, studying intensively together. At the time of the Munich Congresses, the members began to perform plays, first by Edward Schuré, and then Rudolf Steiner's Mystery Plays. This changed the situation to some extent

***Die Weihnachtstagung zur Begründung der Allgemeinen Anthroposophischen Gesellschaft*, Dornach 1963.

English translation of the Foundation Stone and accompanying addresses, *The Foundation Stone*, London 1957.

and began to bring anthroposophical activities before the eyes of the world at large. This happened through the various artistic activities which began to grow up —eurythmy, speech-formation, etc., and through the Goetheanum building, originally planned for Munich, which was being built on the Dornach hill. Even so, only small sections of the public were affected at this time. When the first world war broke out, the members—who were citizens of many different countries—worked together in seclusion around the Dornach hill.

But during the later years of the war, the situation changed. Many—mostly younger—people appeared from different walks of life, wanting to know how Anthroposophy could be carried out into the world and brought to bear on their own work. This trend became more significant when from 1917 on, Rudolf Steiner began to bring forward ideas for a new social order, in an attempt to bring some harmony into the growing chaos of the world at large.

In the late autumn of 1918, as soon as the war ended, Anthroposophy emerged in public, through the High School courses (Hochschulkurse), the great public lectures, and the intense activity in the Threefold Commonwealth Movement. In due course there arose the Freie Waldorfschule, from which the educational work very quickly spread into other countries; at the same time there were attempts to start something new in the economic and business world. These were less successful. This is not the place to describe all these efforts in detail. It is sufficient to emphasise how painful it was for Rudolf Steiner to see how his universal spiritual initiatives were taken up with such inadequate energy and resources. Later he was also sharply critical of the High School work, where there was too much of a tendency to introduce practices strongly influenced by normal high school traditions.

This was, of course, an extraordinarily active and spirit-filled period. In those years Dr. Steiner was giving a great and stimulating variety of lectures, and interest was growing. One felt, nevertheless, that a sort of empty space was developing within the Society, and all kinds of difficulties began to appear. The Goetheanum fire then demonstrated, in a terrible way, the vulnerability of this building, created as it was out of a holy impulse of will.

The following year of 1923 was for many who experienced it one of pain and grief. Representatives of a new generation had now begun to come into the Anthroposophical Movement. But at the Delegates Conference in Stuttgart in 1923, it became evident that their impulses could not find a place in the Society. It became necessary to found a new Society, and so the Free Anthroposophical Society was established, whose statutes were written down by Rudolf Steiner himself.

The year of 1923 was also devoted to preparing an International General Society, as Rudolf Steiner described it at the time. An Anthroposophical Society had existed since 1913. Rudolf Steiner himself did not belong to it, but worked with it—as he often emphasised —simply as a teacher. There were at the time no national societies. In the various countries in which Anthroposophy was represented, the local groups adhered to the central Anthroposophical Society. This had now to change, and the intention was to found independent societies in the different countries. Rudolf Steiner emphasised that these should be autonomous, and he wanted them to be founded and their statutes drawn up before the proposed Christmas Conference. The national societies would then come together freely to form the new General Anthroposophical Society which was to be founded.*

The members continually argued among themselves about what this new Society should be like, but it was difficult at the time to get Rudolf Steiner to say anything about it. He gave the impression that he was waiting to see what would be brought to him from the circles of members in the various countries.

At the Delegates Conference in Dornach in June 1923, which had been called mainly in connection with the question of re-building the Goetheanum, this impression was reinforced. The delegates had hoped to hear something about the proposed International Society, but they

*"Such an International Society can only be founded in Dornach at Christmas if the individual national societies have first come into existence and send their delegates to Dornach. The International Anthroposophical Society can then be founded from out of the national societies. The national societies must be based in one way or another on the Statutes. The national societies will be formed before the foundation of the International Society in Dornach. The International Society must arise on the basis of the national societies."
(From the address by Rudolf Steiner at the Foundation Meeting of the Anthroposophical Society in Holland, 18th November, 1923. Published in *Rudolf Steiner und die Zivilisationsaufgabe der Anthroposophie*, Dornach 1943. (No English translation published).)

heard nothing definite. As a result, efforts were made in different countries to assemble members and generate enthusiasm for the great ideal of a clearly differentiated world Society to include the whole Movement.

There was no conception at that time of the great sacrifice Rudolf Steiner was to make in founding the new Society. Perhaps the first indication was during a meeting in Holland in November 1923, when he expressed deep doubts about whether he could continue to associate himself with the Society. But then, on the next day, in the concluding lecture of the cycle "Supersensible Man, in the Light of Anthroposophy", he spoke of how, during the Goetheanum fire, through the flames of the metal made molten by the heat, it was possible to see deep into the Karma-building forces of man. It was as though he was pointing to the connection between those sacrificial flames and his coming deed at the Christmas Foundation Meeting, when he was to take on the office of President ('Erste Vorsitzender') of the Society and of the Free High School. His personal destiny was to be completely united with that of the Society now coming into being.

From that moment this Society, which was founded at Christmas 1923 in the presence of delegates from the different national societies, could no longer be called an "International Society". It no longer had any direct connection with the nations to which individuals belonged; it was a Society formed out of purely human forces. Immediately after the laying of the Foundation Stone, the representatives of the national societies described the situation in their countries and what they felt about the Christmas Conference. Rudolf Steiner welcomed each personally, and invited them one by one up onto the platform to thank them for their contribution. Thus it became evident that this society of human beings was to be composed of that which was freely contributed from the different countries.

The Laying of the Foundation Stone, 1923

From the way Rudolf Steiner delivered the opening address, beginning by making a special sign, it was immediately apparent that a deed would be performed which would introduce a new phase in the development of the Mysteries of mankind. When the Foundation Stone Meditation had been spoken out, few realised immediately the intimate connection of its contents with that which had begun to live on earth through the laying of the first Foundation Stone and the building of the Goetheanum. On this occasion, the Foundation Stone was laid in the form of a meditation verse into the hearts of those present. Rudolf Steiner emphasised that the sacred goal which was thus set before members could only be reached through their united wills. Seven to eight hundred members were present. Some were there as representatives of national societies, but many were there simply because their destiny had led them to be present. The laying of this Foundation Stone can thus be described as an almost public Mystery deed. For it is certain that not only official representatives of their groups had come, but also others, some of whom had only recently become members, and who could hardly yet have become connected with the actual destiny of the Society on earth.

Rudolf Steiner stood before the members as the High Priest of a new, emergent mankind. The individual souls present, deeply connected through shared experiences before birth, were already dimly aware of their resolution to serve humanity as a whole. Now they could enter into a new spiritual world with increasing clarity of consciousness.

Rudolf Steiner spoke as one who was completely uniting himself with this emerging community, and was placing himself entirely within it. He spoke of the Foundation Stone "World Dodecahedron", and in contrast to it, the "Dodecahedron of Man . . . . . which we lay in the ground of our souls". It was a communal deed which he performed with all those present, not placing himself above or beyond them even while living on the highest plane himself.

The seven or eight hundred members present represented the membership at large. But in a deeper sense, they represented the spiritual quest of modern mankind. They were chosen by destiny to receive the Foundation Stone into their hearts directly from spiritual heights. But they could also feel that those not present—including perhaps those not living on the physical plane, were participating in the laying of this Foundation Stone as well. Certainly many souls in the spiritual world were listening, both the departed and those yet unborn. The Hierarchies—called upon with such great power—listened too.

Later on, when working quietly and meditatively with the Foundation Stone, its resemblance to the Foundation Stone of the first Goetheanum became increasingly clear.

Nevertheless, there was a difference. The human soul could indeed live in the first Goetheanum with its three soul-forces, thinking, feeling and willing; and yet, the threefold membering of the human being, in which the soul reveals itself, was not yet clearly expressed. It only became possible for Rudolf Steiner to perceive this threefold membering of the human organism completely in 1917. He described it for the first time in a chapter of his book, *Riddles of the Soul.* This concept of the threefold membering of the human organism, the description of man's three systems of organs, first gave humanity the opportunity to comprehend scientifically the true relationship between soul and body. At the beginning of the 20th Century, it was still the custom to think in one way or another of a "seat of the soul", and to associate it only with the nerve-and-sense systems. The connection between the three levels of the soul's life—perception and idea-forming, feeling, and willing—and the three systems of organs—the nerves-and-senses system, the rhythmic system, and the metabolic-limb system—had never been grasped. These facts are of immeasurable importance, and the time will come when this revelation will be seen as the true foundation of a knowledge of man. It will unite anatomy, physiology and psychology in a coherent way on the basis of spiritual science. This concept of the threefold man finds its supreme expression in the Foundation Stone of 1923.

In the Foundation Stone address, Rudolf Steiner also indicated, right at the beginning, how this threefold membering had been perceived by him as the foundation of self-knowledge for decades past—but that he had only been able to bring it to maturity "in the past decade, during the storms of war".

For this reason, the Foundation Stone Meditation had three main sections, to which a fourth is added. Each of the three sections has two parts, just as the first Goetheanum with its double cupola, revealed the interplay of the earthly and the spiritual forces of the human soul.

Three times there sounds forth the summons: "Soul of Man!" Then is shown in three groups of three lines each how this soul of man lives in the limbs, in the rhythms of the heart and lungs, and in the resting head. The soul is thereby led to recognise itself in Space, Time and Eternity, just as it was able to experience it in the first Goetheanum building. For it is not physical space into which the human soul wakes when it recognises that it *lives* in the limbs. The world of Space which is meant here is a door leading through to the ocean-being of the Spirit—in other words, to the etheric world. One can also say: When the human soul recognises how it lives unconsciously in the limbs, it feels that these limbs do not belong to the realm of the physical-mechanical forces of our earth. When it moves within the limbs the soul enters into an etheric world.

In the same way, when the individual really *lives* in the rhythm of heart and lungs, he will recognise that he is being led into the realm of Time—and that he then experiences a different world, the world of feeling in his own soul-being. What goes on in the beat of the heart and the rhythm of the lungs is full of secrets. In the functions of heart and lung the eternal alternation of forces of life and death expresses itself. The blood is continually revitalised by the oxygen which is breathed in. And from the consciousness the stream of death-forces enters continually into the blood in the asphyxiating carbon-dioxide. In this way, human feeling becomes a process deeply connected with the Rhythms of the Worlds; it is the breathing process which takes place between the human soul and the soul of the world. In every age it will take on a different character. But man will always feel the relationship experienced in this way as the inmost aspect of his being. As he lives in Space, so he dies into Time. But it is just this dying which leads him to himself.

Man can only fully grasp the meaning of life and death for his spiritual development when he experiences the eternal nature of his being. The Upanishads pointed to this—to how man wakes to his spirit only when he has recognised how life and death alternate with each other as stages of development:—

"*He who knows that growth and decay*
Stand on completely equal footing
Escapes death through decline
And becomes immortal through birth".

Mystics, like Angelus Silesius also know the secrets of life, death and eternity:

"*No death is more glorious than that which brings life,*
"*No life is nobler than that which springs from death.*
"*God himself, when He wills that thou shouldst live, must die:*
"*How shouldst thou inherit His life without death?*"

Man can know life and death profoundly when he devotes himself to the eternal, Universal Thoughts. This becomes possible when he experiences himself in the resting head, of which the third part of the Foundation Meditation speaks.

In the Goetheanum, the soul's experience of Space, Time and Eternity were made visible in form and colour through Imagination: in the Foundation Stone meditation the same experiences are revealed through the powers of Inspiration. In the threefold summons to the human soul one can experience the astonishing fact that Rudolf Steiner was able to take the mighty Imaginations which lived in the Goetheanum building—which then passed through the consuming flames to rise up to spiritual heights—and to bring them back, in the form of Inspirations, as the Foundation Stone Meditation.

Each of the three groups of three opening lines is followed immediately by the three exercises: "Practise Spirit-recollection" ; " Practise Spirit-mindfulness" ; "Practise Spirit-vision". The Foundation Stone is Anthroposophy as it lived in the first Goetheanum building, reborn out of the world of Inspiration; and like the first Goetheanum, it poses tasks. While the Goetheanum was being built, Rudolf Steiner spoke in a lecture of its task. He said that it was a "beautiful, marvellous instrument of education", an instrument "beyond and above everything personal". Earlier, he had said: "How essential—oh, how essential it is to outgrow everything personal if it is to make sense to have forms such as those attempted here as a framework for our work in spiritual science". Just this could be experienced at the Goetheanum; it was impossible to remain as one was; either one behaved as a detached spectator, judging the building from the usual aesthetic points of view and thus remaining outside it; or one really entered into it with the soul and allowed the forms and colours to work on one.

Naturally with most people this process went on almost unconsciously; nevertheless the effect of an environment of such forms and colours was distinctly perceptible.

But now, through the Foundation Stone Meditation, the task was set much more consciously. The human soul can know itself as living in a truly spiritual world of Space, in a truly, spiritually-understood, experience of Time, and in an Eternity comprehended by the spirit. Through this fact, there was called into the soul the necessity to practise these relationships consciously. The three exercises lead man to experience himself in his soul as an Ego. But he learns to know this Ego from three aspects: how it comes to being within the I of God; how it unites itself with the I of the world; and how it rises up to free Willing.

All three exercises are not unfamiliar to those who have studied anthroposophy. One of the first exercises of which Rudolf Steiner speaks in his book *Knowledge of the Higher Worlds* is that of looking back during a moment of inner quiet on the day's experiences. These experiences should be contemplated in the same way as someone walking in the mountains might look back from a height upon the path he has trodden—as a spectator, so to speak. Various looking-back exercises are described:

the survey of the day each evening; looking back at particular phases of one's life, phases which one passed through in childhood, and so on. It should really be possible, after several years of these exercises, to look back on one's whole life as a detached observer.

It can also be said that Anthroposophy as a whole, in so far as it includes descriptions of the birth and development of the earth and mankind—such as those mentioned in *Occult Science*—is in fact an exercise which leads to ever deeper and more comprehensive spirit-recollection. Man learns—even if not fully consciously—to know himself in cultural epochs during which he has lived several lives, and indeed in earlier stages of the earth's evolution altogether, during the Moon, Sun and Saturn stages. Thus the exercise "practise Spirit-recollection" is to be understood in its broadest sense, as an exhortation to penetrate ever further into the depths of the soul, and thereby to recognise the divine powers out of which the human Ego was born. Through practising this verse, a true "living" is achieved in that sphere in which both the world and man were born out of the divine womb (*Gottes-Schoss*).

The second exercise is to practise "Spirit-mindfulness". Here, too, the whole of Anthroposophy is both a prerequisite and a direct way to what is meant. Where "Spirit-recollection" means immersing oneself in the soul's depths, "Spirit-mindfulness" is practised in balance of the soul—that is to say, in inner quiet. Achieving this inner quiet is, as has already been said, one of the first tasks set by the book *Knowledge of Higher Worlds*. The tumult of everyday life must vanish from our souls, the higher man must be born within us. Immediately following the description of inner quiet in the book is a discussion of the nature of meditation. "Spirit-mindfulness" may also be regarded essentially as a meditation. But the concept of meditation is not to be taken in too narrow a sense. Reading and studying Anthroposophy should also gradually be transformed from an intellectual to a more meditative activity, so that the spiritual content may live in the soul. This new way of reading is, in fact, one of the most important exercises in an age which is wholly accustomed to reading with the head.

As the individual becomes, through Spirit-mindfulness, more profoundly aware of his higher being, as his own Ego comes more fully to birth, he also approaches the sphere in which the laws of destiny can be perceived. He will experience those divine-spiritual powers who guide his destiny. Eventually, through the recognition of the laws of destiny he will experience the unification of his higher Ego with the World-Ego, with the Christ. Only then, in the process of unification of his own Ego and the World-Ego there emerges true feeling—feeling that can be described in the truest sense as a breathing process between human Ego and World Ego. Compared to this feeling, the emotions and sensations we normally call feelings are only shadowy replicas.

The third task is to practise "Spirit-vision". This should take place in the quietness of the life of thought. In other words, inner peace is again the starting-point. The whole path of knowledge which Rudolf Steiner described—starting in the 1870s and culminating during that earlier period in the *Philosophy of Spiritual*

Activity—and, indeed, the whole of Anthroposophy, is a path of spiritual practice. In this connection, the 'Leading Thoughts' given by Rudolf Steiner after the Christmas Meeting, and the later Letters to members, are of special importance. What he gave then represents a pinnacle in the entire spiritual life of mankind.

Spirit-vision practised in quietness of thought leads into the sphere in which Michael, as Regent of the cosmic intelligence, shows to human souls, through his gesture of guidance, the way to an inner setting-free of the spirit. The "eternal aims of Gods" endow us with "World-Being's Light", so that the individual Ego can arise to free Willing. Only then does man come to think truly within the "ground of the Spirit in Man". One is reminded here of the words that are already found in *Truth and Knowledge*, where the process of knowing is described as a "steady growth into the ground of worlds".

These three exercises, therefore, lead us to comprehend the constantly unfolding Ego. For one cannot say that the human Ego *is*—only that it is 'becoming'. It can only be grasped in this process of becoming—the Ego in the past, present and future, which comes to being within the I of God, unites itself with the I of the world, and ascends to a freely willing I.

It should be noted that at the beginning of each of the three main sections, it is said of the human soul: "Thou livest"—in the limbs, in the beat of the heart and lungs, in the resting head. In this way it is evident that when the three regions of the human organism are mentioned, it is the functional man who is meant, the man who lives etherically, so to speak, within the physical man.

As already mentioned, the concept of the threefold human being can be regarded as one of the most important concepts of modern knowledge. It is related to Goethe's Idea of the archetypal plant (*Urpflanze*), which is not, as Goethe perhaps originally believed, to be found as a physical reality, but rather, as he later recognised, as a pure Idea from which all plants have sprung in the past and can continue to spring in the future. It is the same with the concept of the threefold man: it is the divine Idea out of which the physical, soul and spiritual organism of man has arisen and will continue to arise. In the Foundation Stone Meditation this Idea finds its highest expression. For the first time in the history of man, an Idea represents exactly the anatomical, physiological and psychological nature of man, and at the same time provides the content for the highest of Meditations.

When the threefold organisation is grasped in this way as a living being, the human soul and the human Ego can unfold within it in a living way.

We have now concerned ourselves with the first part of each of the three main sections of the Meditation. Each of these parts is then followed by a second part. After the summons: "Soul of Man", each of the first parts contains twelve lines. The number twelve is the expression of spatial extension, as in the three times four signs of the Zodiac spread out around us in our solar system. The second part of each section contains seven lines; then come two lines standing by themselves with a particular content. The number seven has to do with development proceeding in rhythm and in time. Indeed the second part of each section can be considered as a bearer of the divine spiritual Inspiration itself. In the first part, the connection is made with the immediate weaving of the human soul within the bodily organism. From there the meditation rises to take hold of the Ego in the world of "becoming".

In the second part of each section, one is concerned with the entire divine-spiritual world of Beings through which this path on earth is made possible. Each part begins with the word "For". This indicates that the task set in the preceding section can only be achieved because the whole evolution of man has its origins in the Trinity, which is the basis of our whole solar system. The Divine Trinity is invoked as the Father-Spirit of the Heights, the Christ-Will in the encircling Round, and as the Spirit's Universal Thoughts.

These are the three powers from out of which, through our common will, the Foundation Stone could be formed: The power of the Father-Spirit, who in the Depths of Worlds begets life, and through the First Hierarchy, the Spirits of Strength, lets ring out from the Heights, the Word which is echoed in the Depths; then the power of the Christ Will, which, working in the encircling round in the Rhythms of the Worlds, blesses the soul, and through the Second Hierarchy brings together the Spirits of Light, with the powers of fire and form, so that life may arise anew from death; thirdly, the power of the Universal Thoughts which live in the Spirit, which crave for Light in the Being of All Worlds, and through the Third Hierarchy, the Spirits of Soul, send up the prayer from the Depths to the Heights through which the souls can awaken in the Spirit's Universal Thoughts.

The word *walten** is heard three times. This word, right into its very sounds, bears within it that which creates, eternally works and generates from out of the spirit. Linked to the divine Trinity are the thrice three choirs of the Hierarchies which, on the occasion of the laying of the Foundation Stone, Rudolf Steiner called upon by their true names; in a version printed afterwards they were called Spirits of Strength, Spirits of Light and Spirits of Soul. The relationship of these thrice three choirs of the Hierarchies to the Foundation Stone as such will be described in the next chapter.

The final lines of each set of seven contains one of the three Rosicrucian sayings. These were originally in their Latin form and then, in print, translated into German and re-formed.

It is difficult to express in words the connections between what sounds in these last lines of the three main sections of the Meditation and what is revealed in the smaller dome of the first Goetheanum, in the Mystery Plays, in Eurythmy, and in Dr. Steiner's lectures; nevertheless, these connections will increasingly reveal themselves to more profound contemplation.

The laying of the Foundation Stone in 1913 began with Rudolf Steiner turning to the four points of the compass, thus giving the building an orientation in the world which was simultaneously anchored in the earth element. So, too, at the end of the main sections of the

*Translated as "holds sway."

verse, there is, each time, the statement that the Elemental Beings in the East, West, North and South hear this voice from the spiritual worlds. Immediately afterwards comes the line: "May human beings hear it".

The fourth main section of the verse again has two parts. To begin with, we are reminded of the moment of time when that event in world-history occurred which is described, quite simply, as the "turning-point of time". Then the "Divine Light", the "Sun of Christ", the "Spirit-Light of the World", entered "the Stream of Earthly Being".

Light of Love and Light of Wisdom together, warming and enlightening, working into the two main streams of humanity, which are expressed in the two Nativity stories in the Gospels.

In the Foundation Stone Meditation, there appears before us in a kind of metamorphosis the wood-carved Christ statue. Christianity approaches us now from spiritual heights, and is only to be grasped through Inspiration. Lucifer and Ahriman are not mentioned, but the powers which can redeem and transform them are—the powers of love and wisdom.

The second part contains a prayer. On entering the first Goetheanum, moving from West to East, the soul could carry within the will an inner prayer that Christ should become increasingly the guide of its being. So too, in the verse, comes the prayer for warmth and light, so that heart and head may be illumined with the Sun of Christ.

As already mentioned, the Foundation Stone was laid in the hearts of those present. It must be laid,

Rudolf Steiner said, "into our hearts that are working together harmoniously, filled with love and good will, striving to bear the anthroposophical impulse through the world". Just as the first Goetheanum rose up out of the forces of the double pentagonal dodecahedron, which was sunk in the foundation stone, so the spiritual edifice of the General Anthroposophical Society and the Free High School was now to grow out of the forces of the Foundation Stone Meditation.

The whole of Anthroposophy passed through a fiery death when the first Goetheanum was burned, and it was reborn in the Foundation Stone Meditation. And one can say that the Society founded at the Christmas Meeting really represented a metamorphosed Goetheanum. But this new spiritual edifice, this transformed Goetheanum, was not confined in space, but arose each time anew wherever human beings sought to work from out of the forces of the Foundation Stone Meditation. A great Mystery took place at the Christmas Foundation Meeting. A seed was sown so that the possibility was created for the world to become a temple, wherever human souls live and work out of the Foundation Stone's power.

From The Philosophers' Stone to the Stone of Love

The Foundation Stone, which was given in the form of a meditation verse on 25th December, 1923, was described by Dr. Steiner in his address as a dodecahedral Foundation Stone of Love—and later, also, simply as a dodecahedral Stone of Love.

The great Mystery of the Christmas Foundation Meeting was preceded by a series of lectures on the Mysteries of ancient times.* The last of these was delivered on 23rd December 1923, and its theme was the Philosophers' Stone. In the Mysteries, Dr. Steiner said, the secret of Gold, Silver and Carbon had been known since very ancient times. Gold represented the Sun, and has a special connection with thinking. "In his thinking, man is quickened by gold". Silver is connected with the Moon, and its forces live in our growth-processes. It builds the living form, and in the plants its activity appears as pure carbon. Carbon is the Philosophers' Stone of the Middle Ages.

It appears in the present earth-evolution in three forms: as diamond it manifests its origin in the Old Sun evolution; as graphite, it still bears within it traces of the Old Moon stage; as plain carbon it retains the formative plant forces of the earth's origins.

* *Mysteriengestaltungen*, fourteen lectures at Dornach, 23rd November to 23rd December 1923. Dornach 1974. English translation, *Mystery Knowledge and Mystery Centres*, Rudolf Steiner Press, London, 1973.

As early as the 8th Century, the alchemists were describing the marvellous powers of this Stone, which they referred to in mysterious terms without revealing that they were speaking of carbon. They said, for instance, that this Stone is to be found everywhere, and yet it is wholly unknown; it is both the lowliest and the noblest, mineral and not mineral, it has a special relationship to fire, etc.

Throughout, the alchemical writings tend to refer to ancient Mysteries, particularly those of Egypt; Hermes is described as the first great alchemist; a certain Maria Hebraeica is often referred to, supposedly the sister of Moses. A name which appears in Goethe's *Faust* also turns up, a certain Dr. Marianus, also referred to as Marianus Christianus. Nearly all the alchemists trace their ideas back to Aristotle, as do a number of learned Arabs like Avicenna. The best known, from the 13th Century onwards are: Albertus Magnus, Thomas Aquinas, Raimundus Lullus, Arnoldus Villanove and several others. Then in the 15th and 16th Centuries there are Basil Valentine, Paracelsus, Van Helmont, Robert Fludd.

It is not easy to find one's way through all these writings, since some have only come down to us after being repeatedly copied, and the copiers have inserted their own commentaries into the text. Those writings which were printed originated much later, and in most cases it is clear that the more recent author is himself no longer clear about the true, original impulse behind the search for the Philosophers' Stone. Thus it is not easy to describe ideas of the various alchemists concerning the Philosophers' Stone and their relationship to our Foundation Stone Meditation.

However, in a little 18th Century book, the Stone is characterised in a remarkable way, and provides us with an important hint. It says there: "This Stone is three-cornered in Esse or Being, four cornered in Quality or Constitution" (*Of a True Adept, Special Secrets of Alchemy*, 1757).

If one takes Esse or Being to mean the First Principles of which alchemy so often speaks, the trinity of Salt, Mercury, Sulphur, then there becomes evident a connection with the three parts of the organism of the threefold man: nerves and senses; rhythmic system; limbs and metabolism.

The fourfold Quality or Constitution points to the four Elements which also played a prominent part in the search for the Philosophers' Stone. In this connection, a kind of poem should be referred to which Rudolf Steiner quoted in an unpublished esoteric lecture (Berlin, 12th February 1908). It is to be found in old Rosicrucian books as he gave it or with some variations:

Wer der Zahlen Wirken wohl durchschaut
Sieht wie seine Welt sich auferbaut.
Die Vier als erste Zahl der Elemente überall,
Aus ihr die Drei sich regen,
Geist, Seele, Leib dir geben,
Die Zwei entsteht aus Sonne und Mond,
Daraus erwächst der Menschen-Sohn

Dem auf der Welt gar nichts gleich,
Der übertrifft all Erdenreich.*

With the verse is a diagram on which are depicted the signs for the four Elements, Earth, Water, Air and Fire; below are the signs for Sulphur, Mercury and Salt; then a hexagram, and right at the bottom a sphere with a cross, symbol of the earth.

These four ancient signs for the Elements, which are found throughout alchemical writings, are genuine occult pictures. Fire is represented as a triangle with the point upwards—the picture of a flame. Air is a triangle with the point upwards and a horizontal line—a sign that Air is made up of a heavy portion, the actual air, and a lighter part, the Light Ether. Water is represented by a triangle with the point down; and Earth by the same triangle with a horizontal line—indicating the process of solidification from out of the liquid state.

As the verse says, the three arise from the four: sulphur is born out of Fire, and is represented by a triangle with the point upwards and a cross below—Fire is thus shown bound to the earth, or working on the earth.

*"He who knows how number weaves
Creation of his world perceives.
The number Four reigns first
O'er the elements dispersed,
The Three arises from it
Giving Body, Soul and Spirit.
The Two is born from Sun and Moon
From which there springs the Son of Man
Upon this earth beyond compare
He has in all the world no peer".
(Trans. J. D.).

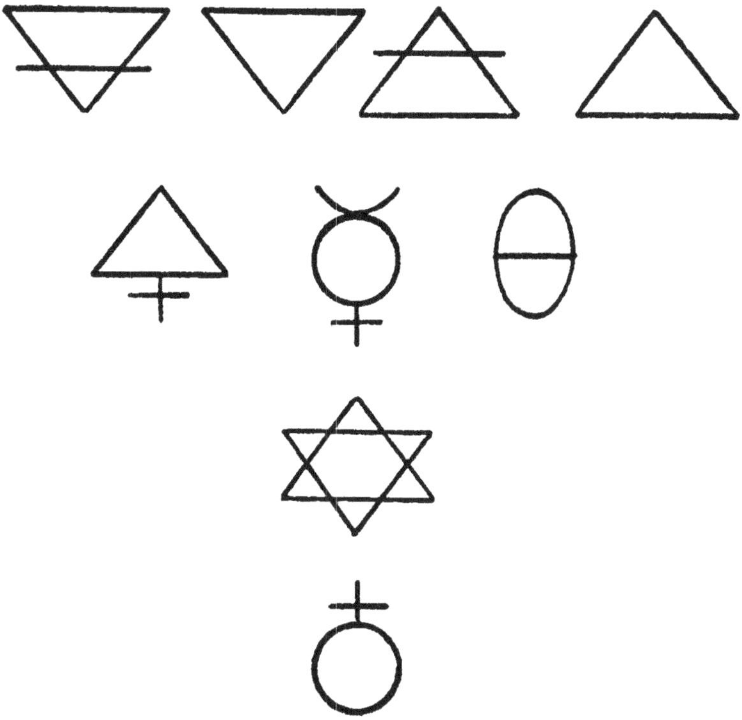

Fig. 1

Salt is shown not as a triangle but as a round drop with a horizontal line across the middle. Sulphur represents for the alchemist all combustion processes,—the ordinary combustion of matter; the inner combustion processes of the metabolism; and also the drives and impulses of will in man and animal. In the same way, Salt represents the processes of crystallisation, hardening and mineralisation. It includes salt which crystallises out of the sea, the skeleton-building processes in man and animal, and everything connected with the conceptual life. Sulphur and Salt can be derived directly from the Elements.

With Mercury, which stands in the middle, the matter is not so simple. As is indicated in the verse, there is a duality in Mercury. The sign is the same as that for the planet, a Moon and Sun sign together, anchored in the earth through the small cross beneath the Sun symbol. This points to something in man himself which is hard to understand—the middle part of threefold man. Where two polarities meet, a centre arises; but it is more important to realise how the central part of the being of man was implicit and intended from the first:

"The two arise from Sun and Moon
"From which doth spring the Son of Man"

the Rosicrucian verse says. This points to the highest goal of man's evolution—to bring Christ to birth within himself. Man is represented in the diagram by a hexagram, a regular six-cornered figure in which the four signs of the Elements can be recognised.

Now let us consider the Foundation Stone Meditation. At the end come the words: "The Spirits hear it in East and West and North and South . . . . " It is certainly of deep significance that during the Christmas period of 1923 Rudolf Steiner twice spoke of the nature of the Elements as Aristotle, for instance, had taught it to his pupil Alexander. He spoke of this on December 15th in the afore-mentioned lectures on the Mysteries, and then again, during the Christmas meeting, in an evening lecture on December 27th 1923. Rudolf Steiner describes how the Elements can be experienced in relation to the four points of the compass and their special characters. He spoke not only of Earth, Water, Air and Fire, but also of their combinations which lead to the conditions of cold, warm, dry and wet. Cold arises where Water and Earth are at work; dry from the activity of Earth and Fire; warmth from the activity of Fire and Air; and wet from the activity of Air and Water.

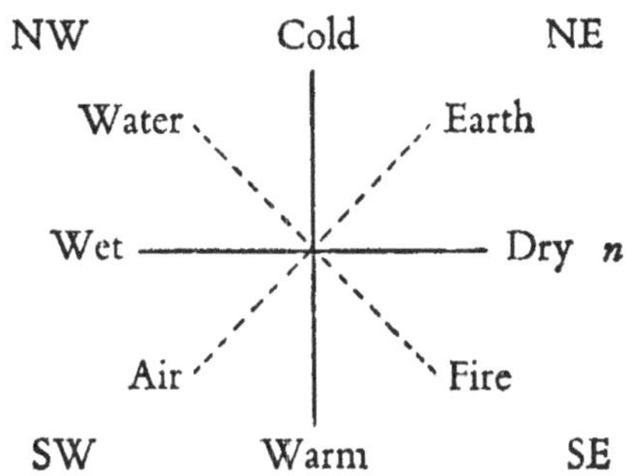

Fig. 2

Inwardly experienced, this reveals to man his fourfold nature, physical body, etheric body, astral body and Ego. In the lectures there are described the tragic feelings of the alchemists of the Middle Ages as they saw how an immediate relationship to the spiritual world, to the Hierarchies and to the Trinity, was no longer possible. Only the spirits of the Elements, the Elemental Beings, still appeared to them in their experiments. It was still known, in the Middle Ages, how the Elements are connected with the human organism. There is, for instance, a saying attributed to Raimundus Lullus: "The Warm and Dry draws to itself", and there he puts the sign for Fire, that is, for the Ego. "The Dry and Cold holds to itself"—and there is the sign for Earth, that is, for the physical body. "Cold and Wet drives out" is accompanied by the sign for Water, or etheric body. And "Wet and Warm consumes" goes with the sign for Air, or astral body. In such a saying, an entire physiology is contained in a condensed form.

In December 1923, Rudolf Steiner spoke twice about the nature of the Elements in order to indicate how important it is for men today to understand once more the forces of the Elemental world and their working in our whole being.

In three lectures on December 17th, 18th and 19th, 1920, he had already pointed to these important connections, to the Elements, the different members of the human being, the forces of the soul, etc., in relation to man's moral will and striving for freedom.*

Now let us consider, once more, the three main sections of the Foundation Stone. We see that the connection with the three "vital" alchemical principles, Sulphur, Mercury and Salt, emerges clearly. Man lives in his limbs; there, his metabolic processes are brought to completion. Sulphur works in the constant transformation of those processes which carry the unconscious will-forces. The power of memory is also intimately connected with these Sulphur forces.

When one thinks of the life-begetting forces which work from the Father Spirit into the depths of worlds, one encounters Sulphur as a heavenly power. It is the divine Power of Love which is also at work in the three choirs of the First Hierarchy. The Seraphim are the

* *Die Brücke zwischen der Weltgeistigkeit und dem Physischen des Menschen*, Dornach 1970. English translation, *The Bridge Between Universal Spirituality and the Physical Constitution of Man*, New York, 1979.

Spirits of Love. It is the creative love of the Gods which works as a fiery glow. One can understand that it was an ideal of the mystics "to be consumed in the glow of seraphic love".

In a lecture given on 14th March 1908 in Berlin, Rudolf Steiner again quotes a verse which can be found in Rosicrucian writings:

"Strive for the fire, seek for the fire,
"Thou shalt become fire.
"Bring fire to fire, broil fire in fire,
"Throw body, soul and spirit into fire,
"Then hast thou dead and living fire,
"Thou shalt become black, yellow, white, red fire
"Bear thy children in fire,
"Give them food and drink in fire,
"Thus they live and die in fire,
"Their silver and gold shall all become fire
"And shall be in the end a fourfold philosophic fire"

Rudolf Steiner explains what is meant by the "fourfold philosophic fire". In the black fire, Old Saturn begins, in which all is warmth but gives out no light; in the yellow fire is the Old Sun, where light is already shining forth; the white fire refers to the Old Moon, when it becomes an inner stream of sap in living beings; the red fire refers to the Earth condition when it works in the blood.

But not only the Seraphim reveal the fiery love of the Father-Spirit. The Cherubim, too, who penetrate growing creation, work out of the same fire of love. Their harmony-creating wisdom is at the same time true love. The Thrones are the bearers of love which has become will. Their love becomes the power of sacrifice from which the original warmth of Old Saturn can arise.

The first part of the Foundation Stone verse is thus wholly imbued with the Sulphur-power; it shows itself both in human processes and in the working of the divine-spiritual Beings.

In a similar way, the third part is formed wholly out of the Salt forces. Man needs the resting head, of which calcium carbonate and phosphate form the covering. The brain rests within this covering, isolated from the influences of the surrounding world. Even when the head moves, seen spiritually it is at rest. Rudolf Steiner once compared it jokingly with a man being driven around in a carriage who, although moving, regards the world from a position of rest. The mineralisation of the head is necessary for man in order to achieve a genuinely free thinking. Our head system bears the strongest imprint of the purely physical. In the limbs, the Ego, astral and etheric bodies are still connected with the physical body, but their connection with the head is tenuous; only the etheric body has sufficient connection with the nerves and senses to prevent them from dying. But conscious development towards free thinking is only possible because the Ego and astral body have to a large extent separated from the physical body.

Salt appears on earth in its varied crystal forms—and in the spiritual world, too, it presents a marvellous appearance. At the sight of a very large group of quartz crystals, Rudolf Steiner is said to have remarked: "that is what the Devachanic world looks like". Plato said: "God constantly geometrises". Pythagoras and his pupils, and particularly the Platonists, knew of the pure number of relationships which revealed themselves to them as music of the spheres, and which still appear to us in the wonderful forms of crystals.

The central part of the Foundation Stone Meditation is connected with Mercury. The two-fold character of Mercury, in which Sun and Moon meet harmoniously, has already been indicated. It is a force which is concerned above all to assert its own nature. A drop of quicksilver can be divided into ever tinier droplets, all equally round; and they can all just as easily run together to form a big drop. Mercury provides an eloquent, convincing picture of the way a divine unity and multiplicity can arise, all the parts resembling the original unity. This also points towards another fact which has already been mentioned: there lives in Mercury something of an original Principle, not derived from anything else, but which exists through itself alone. In the address given by Dr. Steiner in connection with the Foundation Stone Meditation, are some remarkable words, on which one can ponder long. He speaks of the wonderful secret "that prevails as between Heart and Lung," and of "the World-Rhythms working through centuries and millennia, throughout the Aeons, which beat into the rhythms and pulsing of the blood, ensouling Man from the great Universe." Here, then, is something which expresses itself quite simply and is experienced by everyone in the functioning of heart and lung, and is at the same time deeply connected with that which enables us to be ensouled beings. The inner world of man's soul is continuously blessed by Christ-Will, which works in the encircling round. In this connection, the alchemist speaks of the "Double-Mercury", and represents the dual nature of man in the picture of a divine being bearing the sign of Mercury in both the right and the left hand. Now and again this Double Mercury is also described by the alchemists as the Christ.

Christ works for the whole of mankind: He reveals Himself in the world-rhythms and leads the Fire forces from the East to the Form forces of the West. By moving thus, in this stream from East to West, the forces of death, which work as forces of form out of the West, are overcome through higher forces of life.

Now let us look again at the Rosicrucian verse mentioned earlier (see p. 53). It describes there how the Son of Man arises from Sun and Moon. In Him are revealed love and wisdom interpenetrating. Similarly, the fourth part of the Foundation Stone Meditation is a description of how the Christ Being, the Spirit-Light of the World, came to earth and how that Light gives forth both light and warmth.

The "Philosophic Stone" is completed, as we saw, with a hexagram, a regular hexagon. The sign of the hexagram is a profound expression of the nature of man. Rudolf Steiner once gave another Rosicrucian verse, for meditation, so to speak, in hexagram-form, in the attitude of the hexagram: "Light streams upwards, Weight bears downwards". At the same time, the arms were to be spread upwards, and the legs straddled below, representing the two triangles.*

The Foundation Stone, laid in the earth in 1913 in the form of a pentagonal dodecahedron, is built up entirely on the pentagram and pentagon. Twelve five-sided surfaces come together from the twelve directions of the Universe to form the dodecahedron. Thus the path from the Philosopher's Stone to the Stone of Love involves a very significant metamorphosis, a metamorphosis from the hexagram to the pentagram. The hexagram is well-known as a picture of the Moon forces. Flowers like lilies and all *Liliaceae*, which are connected with the Moon, reveal in cross-section a regular hexagon. Flowers springing from the Sun forces, the wild rose and all the *Rosaceae*, are built up on the pentagram. In the last part of *Occult Science* it says that the Old Moon was a Cosmos of Wisdom, and therefore lies behind everything which is imbued with wisdom on earth. But our earth is to become a Cosmos of Love. The development of the Ego leads from wisdom to love. In *Occult Science*, Rudolf Steiner says: "Love is the result of wisdom reincarnated in the Ego".

If we now look at the two diagrams, the pentagram is, so to speak, a hexagram made inward. When the eurythmists, for example, move round a hexagram, they must move round the outside of the form each time to reach a new starting-point. But the eurythmist who forms the pentagram does not need to move round it but remains within the form, builds it from within.

* *Mysterienstätten des Mittelalters*, Dornach 1980.

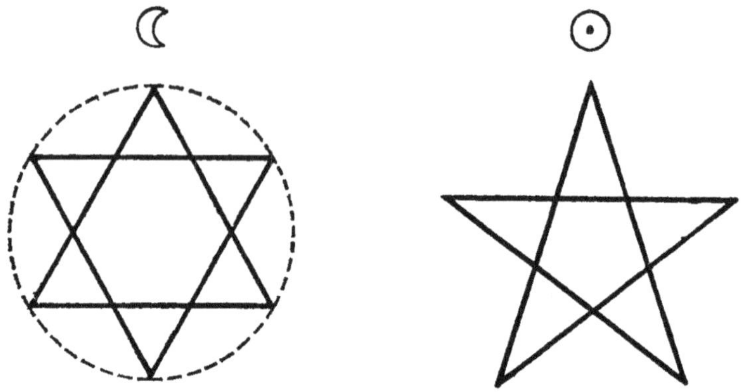

The Ego without The Ego within

Fig. 3

This fact puts before your eyes what occurred when, through the Mystery of Golgotha, the earth received its true meaning: The Ego is no longer outside the other members of man's body, but interpenetrates them. It would be a wonderful meditation to imagine how the hexagram can metamorphose into a pentagram, and at the same time to experience both the pain of the process and the harmony which emerges when the figure is perfected.

This is how it was among the old alchemists. They lived and worked out of an ancient connection with the laws of spiritual evolution; from out of their spiritual quest there began to emerge, at a certain time, an awareness that the Philosophers' Stone was to become the Body of Christ. Some alchemists—for example Raimundus Lullus—expressed how their heart's whole purpose was to prepare the higher body which Rudolf Steiner called the Phantom.*

Their quest found fulfilment when Rudolf Steiner actually achieved the transformation of the Philosophers' Stone into the Stone of Love, the Foundation Stone. The Foundation Stone Meditation, therefore, is a continuous exercise directed to awakening, through spiritual meditation, the pure forces of love in our threefold being.

*C. G. Jung, *Psychology and Alchemy*. Jung indicates that Raimundus Lullus was the first to point to the Lapis-Christus connection. He also mentions others such as Khunrath, and Jacob Boehme.

The Seven Rhythms

The Foundation Stone was laid on Tuesday, 25th December, 1923. The morning meetings on the seven subsequent days always began with Rudolf Steiner reading parts of the Foundation Stone Meditation. He then went on to speak about particular rhythms which connected the individual lines of the meditation with each other. These short addresses and the rhythms which go with them have all been published so that they do not need to be given here in full.

Since then, it has often been asked what the deeper reasons were for the way these rhythms were put together. Naturally, there is much to be found in them. Here an attempt will be made to say something about the inner structure of the rhythms themselves, starting from the thought that the entire Foundation Stone Meditation can create in us a new spiritual body.

Such a spiritual body has, of course, its own subtle membering, and is called forth in the different spheres of consciousness through an inner activity of the Ego. Thus it is not surprising that on the first day—*Wednesday, 26th December*—the three exercises of Spirit-recollection, Spirit-mindfulness, and Spirit-vision are emphasised. They are to be meditated together with those words which refer to the Ego: with Spirit-recollection, the words: "Thine own I comes to being within the I of God";

with Spirit-mindfulness, "Thine own I unite unto the I of the world"; with Spirit-vision, "On thine own I bestow for thy free willing".

Rudolf Steiner emphasised that a moral feeling can be experienced if one comprehends the progression from "come to being", through "unite" to "bestow". To conclude the short address, he said that there was contained in the inner rhythm that "which the Spiritual World is actually bringing to us at this time to lift up our hearts, to illumine our thinking, to bring winged enthusiasm to our will".

The three Ego experiences described above—the experience of the Ego as something developing continuously out of the past, through the present and into the future—are here so placed in the centres of consciousness that one feels one's head, heart and will lifted up through them to one's Higher Ego, which then follows its further path through the whole Foundation Stone Meditation.

Thursday, 27th December. To begin with, the first part of the meditation was read. The starting-point for the rhythms was again the three Ego experiences: "Thine own I comes to being within the I of God"; "Thine own I unite unto the I of the world; "On thine own I bestow for thy free willing". Then were spoken the words: "Then in the All-World-Being of Man thou wilt truly live"; "Then mid the weaving of the Soul of Man thou wilt truly feel"; "Then from the ground of the Spirit in Man thou wilt truly think". The Ego, it may be remembered, brings about the transformation of the astral body, and creates the different members of the soul. True self-knowledge depends on the transformation of the powers of the soul. Through these rhythms it is possible to penetrate deeply into the fundamental structure of the soul. Truly live, truly feel, truly think; this means to bring forth the pure soul-forces through the activity of the Ego. By such activity, the astral body of man is purified; it becomes, as Rudolf Steiner says, a Virgin Sophia. Through such purification, it becomes Manas, or Spirit-Self. Only in such a transformed astral body can one truly live, truly feel and truly think—for only then does one enter the realm of those forces in which man and cosmos interpenetrate in harmony.

At the end of the address given in this connection, Rudolf Steiner said that in such a meditation there should be experienced "utterances of the great secrets of the World, inasmuch as these secrets of the World are resurrected—to become human Self-knowledge—in the soul of Man".

It may be remarked that Steiner here speaks of truly living, truly feeling, and truly thinking—and not, as might be expected, of truly willing. This is because we are still concerned, at this point, with those forces which work as unconscious will-forces in the human organism, that is, as life-forces. It will be remembered that the word "willing" appears later in connection with the thinking. In the third main section, the phrase "truly think" is preceded by "on thine own I bestow for thy free Willing". This points to a secret: that which is called will in ordinary life lives quite hidden in the life-forces, which express themselves in the soul as desires and passions. Only when man has recognised the possibility of freedom, the Will as such is born, and reveals itself spiritually united with the thinking.

Friday, 28th December, began with a reading of the first part of each of the three main sections, together with the two opening lines of the second part:

"For the Father-Spirit of the Heights holds sway
In Depths of Worlds begetting Life".

"For the Christ-Will in the encircling Round holds sway
In the Rhythms of the Worlds, blessing the Soul".

"For the Spirit's Universal Thoughts hold sway
In the Being of all Worlds, craving for Light".

To these lines were added the Rhythms given at the beginning: Practise Spirit-recollection, practise Spirit-mindfulness, practise Spirit-vision. In the address, Rudolf Steiner indicated that these connections are heard in the World-Rhythms. "Practise Spirit-recollection" is an activity "which can take place in the individual soul. It corresponds to that in the great Universe which is expressed in the words: "For the Father-Spirit of the Heights holds sway . . . etc." Answers also come from the great Universe in response to the other exercises.

What does this mean? When, through the exercises, the Ego penetrates ever deeper into the hidden parts of the human being, it experiences the etheric body through the astral body. It should be emphasised that the etheric is not experienced inwardly in the same way as the astral with its different soul-members. Rudolf Steiner, especially in the last years of his life, often pointed to the law of turning-inside-out (*Umstülpung*). The forces of the physical body are centripetal, oriented towards the centre point of the earth. But if the etheric is to be recognised, attention must be directed to those centrifugal forces which work from out of the cosmos. The astral body, on the other hand, has a tendency to close in on itself, because it provides the human soul with an inward self-contained life. But when the Ego breaks through to the etheric forces, it suddenly experiences a kind of turning-inside-out from earthly into cosmic existence. That is why, after the threefold exhortation to meditate, there follows a reply from the universe. Through this the human being is led from his individual Ego to the Ego-power of mankind as a whole as it lives in the cosmos. As physical man, one can feel separate from one's fellow men, but not as etheric man. Although the forces of the human being's own etheric body represent a link with the individual Ego, the etheric nevertheless spans and penetrates mankind as a whole. In the etheric, we are already on the way to becoming humanity. When the etheric body is transformed by the Ego into Life-Spirit (Budhi), then a stage has been reached in which the human being is no longer merely an individual but simultaneously bears within him those forces which enable him to unite with mankind as a whole.

One can thus see how, in these first three rhythms, the Ego is summoned to achieve a higher knowledge of its own nature through the three exercises mentioned, and by taking hold of the forces of the astral body, transforming them to Spirit-Self (Manas), and then penetrating still deeper into the etheric body, transforming it into Life-Spirit (Budhi).

On Saturday, 29th December, the first part of each of the three main sections was again read, together with the second part as far as the Rosicrucian sayings. In the rhythm, the three exercises are again given, and their connection described with the three Hierarchies whose nine choirs are called upon by name. To the first Hierarchy there sound forth the words: "Let there ring out from the Heights what in the Depths is echoed". To the second: "Let there be fired from the East what through the West is formed". To the third: "Let there be prayed in the Depths what from the Heights is answered".

Now the Ego proceeds through the three exercises back to the earliest beginnings of human evolution. Here one may imagine how the human spirit lived during the earliest part of the Old Saturn evolution, still unborn within the Imaginations, Inspirations and Intuitions of the Divine Beings. Right at the beginning, the foundation of the physical body was built up out of all the forces of the universe, in order that in the far future, at the end of the whole cycle of evolution, the Spirit-Man might arise. In this rhythm, the ninefold nature of the world of the Hierarchies as a revelation of the Divine Trinity is given as a path of meditation for the Ego. The purpose is to recognise that the physical body is built up from the most exalted spiritual forces, and that once these are recognised, the Ego may transform them into the highest element of human nature, which in the distant future will become the Spirit Man (Atman).

On Sunday, 30th December, the first parts of the three main sections were again read. Then came the three exercises, followed by the whole of the fourth main section: "At the turning-point of Time . . . . ". The rhythm, written on the blackboard, comprised the three exercises together with the last lines of the fourth main section: "That good may become what from our Hearts we would found and from our Heads direct with single purpose". It has already been pointed out that this fourth main section of the Meditation has quite a different tone from the three preceding ones. These three contain a tremendous ascent into the divine world of the Hierarchies—whereas the fourth main section sounds like a simple story or legend. This legend ends in a prayer. The words are chosen with such simplicity that it is difficult to imagine anything simpler, and yet in them the inmost being of the whole world is expressed.

In the rhythm, there are only two prayers, directed to head and heart, "that good may become what from our Hearts we would found and from our Heads direct with single purpose".

This rhythm leads not only to the Mystery of Golgotha, which took place at the turning-point of time, but beyond it to those preparatory deeds of the Christ Being which took place during the Old Sun evolution. Then the attention is directed to the two streams which appear on the physical plane as the stream of the Kings and the stream of the Shepherds, as is depicted in the two nativity stories in the Gospels. In the concluding words, this is gathered into a profound inward prayer of the human soul that in the future, this Sun of Christ may shape humanity.

This rhythm makes the Christmas festival into more than a festival of remembrance of the birth of the Light of the World; it brings to the human soul an experience of a World-Christmas which leads from the original Sun-condition of the earth, through the Mystery of Golgotha, and points to a time when the Earth will again become Sun. In Christian Morgenstern's words: "That thou, too, may in time become Sun". The Foundation Stone Meditation is designed to provide the inner forces for this purpose.

On Monday, 31st December, the first part of each of the three main sections was again read, and then the fourth main section. The rhythm given was: "O Light Divine, O Sun of Christ"—"The Elemental Spirits hear it in East and West and North and South. May human beings hear it".

This time, the address was quite short. Rudolf Steiner spoke of how this "Light Divine, this Sun of Christ, both shine so that they can be heard like shining suns from East, West, North, South". One is reminded immediately of Goethe's reference to the sounding sun ("tönende Sonne")! Rudolf Steiner here points to the fact that the Sun of Christ is heard by the Elemental Beings as a shining Sun from East, West, North, South. It is stated that they hear it. Christ united Himself with the earth through the Mystery of Golgotha. He lives in the etheric world, in which the Elemental Spirits are present as living beings. They have already apprehended the Mystery of Golgotha. May human beings hear it! That is the task which this rhythm sets us: to come to know the world of Nature interwoven with the Light of Christ, and there to learn to understand this Light as the creative Word of a newly evolving Earth.

On Tuesday, 1st January, the first part of each of the

three main sections was again read, together with the corresponding second part as far as the Rosicrucian sayings; then Rudolf Steiner impressed, as he said, "a simple rhythm into our souls". After what had preceded it, this rhythm was indeed quite simple. Each of the three lines—"Thou livest in the Limbs", "Thou livest in the beat of Heart and Lung", "Thou livest in the resting Head", were linked to the opening lines of the second part of the three main sections: "For the Father-Spirit of the Heights holds sway in the Depths of Worlds begetting Life"; "For the Christ-will in the encircling Round holds sway in the Rhythms of the Worlds, blessing the Soul". "For the Spirit's Universal Thoughts hold sway in the Being of all Worlds, craving for Light". If these rhythms are allowed to work on one, the inward birth of the new man may be felt, the future man, threefold, as we have seen, and living wholly in the etheric. It is the body which the threefold etheric man will be able to use in the future, and which will be an organ in which the Etheric Christ can live. It is the threefold man born out of the forces of the Trinity.

These brief descriptions may have indicated already that there was a profound inner connection between the rhythms and the days on which they were given. Without wishing to define these connections too rigidly, it may be indicated that the fact that the actual laying of the Foundation Stone took place on a Tuesday had a deep significance. The might, the greatness and the wisdom of the whole first half of the Earth-evolution—the Mars-phase—cooperated to prepare the path for those forces which since the Mystery of Golgotha are leading over into the second half of the Earth-evolution, the Mercury-phase. On the Wednesday, that in man which corresponds to these Mercury forces was addressed. The Thursday brought an indication of the transformation of the astral body into Manas, which can only be fully completed in the coming Jupiter-evolution. On Friday, the Venus-evolution was indicated, in which the etheric body will be transformed into Budhi. On the Saturday, Rudolf Steiner indicated that which Vulcan—the new Saturn—will bring, namely the Spirit-Man (Atman), or transformed physical man. The Sunday brought the rhythm which showed to us the Sun Mystery itself, while on the Monday were heralded the ancient forces of wisdom, which are still at work in the Elemental world, transformed by Christ. Finally, the Tuesday brought a return to the original beginnings, when the meaning of the Foundation Stone Meditation was displayed in an extremely simple rhythm, but one which is intended to bring forth within us the new body of the future man.

The Lord's Prayer

One of the deeper—perhaps the very deepest—aspect of the Foundation Stone emerges when its connection with the Lord's Prayer is considered.

The Lord's Prayer is the original prayer of Christianity. It has been prayed for many centuries by millions of people in all moods, pious devotion, thankfulness, fear and despair, in pain and need, by educated people and simple peasants, by members of black and white races. For all of them it has been the prayer that has joined their souls with the heavenly powers. Its words are simple and its esoteric meaning is infinitely profound.

As early as 1907, Rudolf Steiner gave a lecture on the Lord's Prayer.* On that occasion, he touched on the deeper connections between meditation and prayer. Around that time, he had been speaking frequently about evil, the meaning of suffering, illness and death. In his consideration of the Lord's Prayer, he indicated that the whole structure of the prayer is based on a Pythagorean figure, the triangle and the square. In the triangle, which stands above the square, the most exalted powers of the world are represented, the divine Trinity of Father, Son and Holy Spirit, which as yet are only present in man,

* *Das Vaterunser. Eine esoterische Betrachtung*, lecture given on 28th January 1907. Dornach 1976. English translation, *The Lord's Prayer*, London, 1958.

as the germs of Atma, Budhi and Manas. After the opening—"Our Father, Who art in the Heavens"—come the lines— "Hallowed be Thy Name, Thy Kingdom come, Thy Will be done", corresponding to the Holy Spirit, Son and Father—in the Manas, Budhi and Atma of man. Then the transition can be made from the heavens to earth, because in Lemurian times the Ego, which until then had been kept in the divine heights, was implanted into man. In the square, which stands beneath the triangle, follow the four petitions. It was of great significance when Rudolf Steiner, in the above-mentioned lecture, linked the four petitions to the four members of man: physical body, etheric body, astral body and Ego. In this way, the words of these petitions reveal their true meaning. He indicates that the physical body is actually a kind of gateway through which the physical substances of the earth go and are thereby transformed. He often emphasised that in the course of seven years the entire physical substance of the human body is renewed. That which was within us ten years ago is now in external Nature, and other substance has entered. The petition for daily bread refers to this continuous process whereby substances stream through us which belong to divine nature and in which we are constantly immersed.

The second petition, "Forgive us our trespasses, as we forgive them that trespass against us" refers to the etheric body, through which man exists not only for himself, but is connected with his human surroundings, his family, his nation, his contemporaries. The etheric body is the bearer of tendencies and habits, and when man makes an error in this sphere, Rudolf Steiner says, he becomes a sinner within the circle of his fellow human beings, whereas individual sins are committed more through the astral body. "In all occult science, that which is a sin against the community, which flows from the erring etheric body, has always been called trespass."

The third petition, "Lead us not into temptation", is directly connected with the astral body. It is just in the astral body that the forces of temptation are constantly to be found, because, through the Fall, the astral body was given an apparent independence.

The fourth petition, "Deliver us from the evil", refers directly to the Ego, because this Ego is directly attacked by those forces which could move in when man became independent. It is egotism that works in the Ego. "In occult science, the word 'evil' is never used except in reference to an error deriving from the Ego. Evil is thus error from out of the Ego, trespass is error committed by the etheric body in social life, in the life with other human beings. Temptation is that which the astral body can encounter in so far as it errs in an individual personal way. The physical body constantly takes up physical substances for nourishment and thus supports its existence".

It has already been indicated that when the first Foundation Stone was laid in 1913, Rudolf Steiner first gave the Macrocosmic Lord's Prayer as part of the Fifth Gospel. In a lecture in October 1913*, he describes in a moving way how Jesus of Nazareth, in his twenty-fourth year, came to a place where a heathen cult centre had been. The priests had long ago deserted it, and the people

*op.cit. See footnote p.24.

lived on there sick and weakly. As his soul was taken hold of by infinite love, the people urged him to the sacrificial altar, and demanded that he should perform the sacrifice, so that the blessing of God should once more be upon them. Rudolf Steiner described how Jesus of Nazareth fell down as though dead, his soul felt as though separated from the body and lifted up into spiritual worlds, and he heard words which came from a kind of transformed voice of the Bath-Kol. What he heard were the words of the Macrocosmic Lord's Prayer:

"AUM, Amen!
Es walten die Übel,
Zeugen sich lösender Ichheit,
Von andern erschuldete Selbstheitschuld,
Erlebet im täglichen Brote,
In dem nicht waltet der Himmel Wille,
Da der Mensch sich schied von Eurem Reich
Und vergass Euren Namen,
Ihr Väter in den Himmeln".*

*AUM, Amen!
The Evils hold sway,
Witness of Egoity becoming free,
Selfhood-Guilt through others incurred,
Experienced in the Daily Bread,
Wherein the Will of the Heavens does not rule,
In that Man severed himself from Your Kingdom,
And forgot Your Names,
Ye Fathers in the Heavens.

(From *The Fifth Gospel*, five lectures given in Christiana, 1st to 6th October, 1913, trans. D. S. Osmond with the help of M. Cotterell, Rudolf Steiner Press, London, 1978.)

Later, when Christ was with the Apostles, he was able to transform the Macrocosmic Lord's Prayer, because the time had now come when man had himself to travel the path from below upwards, so to speak, into the spiritual world. And so he transformed every line of the prayer, beginning with the last line. Man was no longer to address himself to the spiritual Hierarchies, but to the one Spirit Being who was to be called Father. Thus the Lord's Prayer arose, directly after the Sermon on the Mount.

When Rudolf Steiner laid the Foundation Stone of the General Anthroposophical Society in 1923, the actual Mystery act, as has already been mentioned, was the speaking of the Foundation Stone Meditation. It is a Meditation which is as deep as it is comprehensive, but its conclusion is simultaneously formed as a prayer. The seven primal connections which exist between man and the world, and which are addressed in both the Macrocosmic and the Microcosmic Lord's Prayer, are present as a double trinity. They only reappear as such in the seven rhythms.

The numerical structure of the Foundation Stone Meditation is also important: Opening summons, "Soul of Man", spoken three times, is followed each time by twelve lines. Then, in the subsequent macrocosmic sections come thrice seven lines, to which are added, each time, three lines concerning the Elemental beings and man. The fourth section consists of thirteen (=12+1) and twelve lines. This structure is not unimportant, since in the Meditation these intimate numerical laws also imprint themselves in the etheric.

When the full meaning of the Foundation Stone of 1913 and 1923 is experienced, the question of their relation to the Lord's Prayer naturally arises. It appears almost as a matter of course that the Lord's Prayer should also be contained there. For the Foundation Stone Meditation is an exercise for a community of human beings which is to weave together microcosmic and macrocosmic laws in accordance with the Christianity that is to come.

Following what has been said in the previous chapter about the seven rhythms, the connection is easy to see: the seven rhythms correspond in their succession to the seven lines of the Macrocosmic Lord's Prayer. While the whole Foundation Stone Meditation is built up on the three exercises of Spirit-Recollection, Spirit-Mindfulness, Spirit-Vision, in the rhythms the transforming forces are also addressed that are to bring about the development of the higher members of man. After the Ego, by means of the exercises, has been recognised in its threefold connection with past, present and future, the astral body and Manas, etheric body and Budhi, and physical body and Atma are raised into consciousness.

Now let us consider the Macrocosmic Lord's Prayer in connection with the Microcosmic Lord's Prayer and the petition "Deliver us from the evil". The first rhythm, as we have seen, is concerned with an understanding of the Ego, which is the member of man that encounters evil.

The second line, "Zeugen sich lösender Ichheit" corresponds to the petition "Lead us not into temptation". The second rhythm is concerned with the fact that the

Ego works into the astral body and leads to true living, feeling and thinking, and through this the birth of Manas is prepared. The astral body is freed from the powers of the tempter.

The next line, "Von andern erschuldete Selbstheitschuld" corresponds to the petition "Forgive us our trespasses, as we forgive them that trespass against us". The third rhythm reveals its connection with the etheric body in that through it we experience the cosmic aspect of the etheric within ourselves, since with this rhythm one passes straight over to the first lines of the macrocosmic parts of the verses. (Compare P.69). In this way, one enters into the extra-terrestrial, etheric laws.

Then comes the line "Erlebet im täglichen Brote" which is transformed into "Give us this day our daily bread". In the fourth rhythm, we are given the possibility of experiencing the physical body in its original form as well as in its future being as Atma.

After these four petitions follow the three lines concerning Will, Kingdom, and Name. First comes the line "In dem nicht waltet der Himmel Wille", which is transformed into "Thy Will be done". One enters the realm of the Father. The fifth rhythm, which belongs to it, brings in the turning-point of time as such, that is, one is reminded of the fact that the Son descends to earth and joins the human soul again to the Father. It reveals the true relationship that exists between the Soul, the Son and the Father. In particular, in the High Priestly prayer, Christ asks the Father to receive from him the souls which he has led.

"Da der Mensch schied von Eurem Reich" corresponds to the transformation "Thy Kingdom come". The Kingdom is the realm of the Son. The sixth rhythm shows us that this Kingdom has already arrived on earth: "Light Divine, Sun of Christ". Then one meditates the words: "The Elemental Spirits hear it in East and West and North and South: May human beings hear it!" Rudolf Steiner adds in his address that the light-giving Suns can be heard from East and West and North and South.

The last line, "Und vergass Euren Namen, Ihr Väter in den Himmeln" is transformed into "Hallowed be thy name". This is the world of the Spirit. One may remember here that in the seventh rhythm, Rudolf Steiner gave, as he said, a very simple rhythm. He places before us the picture of threefold man as a perfect balance of the three soul members with the powers of Father, Son and Holy Spirit. In these six lines, man appears in balance between microcosm and macrocosm, threefold in nature and spirit, borne by the Trinity as an expression of the Divine Creative Will. In this way, he can receive his true name, and speaks it in that he speaks out the Name of the Godhead.

In this way, the whole Lord's Prayer is contained in the seven rhythms of the Foundation Stone.

Concerning the Nature of the Foundation Stone

In his address, Rudolf Steiner characterised the Foundation Stone as a "dodecahedral, Imaginative Form of Love" which can shine out before the eye of the soul: "That Foundation Stone which receives from the Universal and human Love its substance, from the Universal and human Imagination its living picture-quality and form, and from the Universal and human Thoughts its radiating Light. And then at all times—if we are mindful of this present moment, the light of it will ray into our hearts, spurring on our action, kindling our thinking, our feeling and our willing".

The connection may be noted here between the three forces mentioned by Steiner which make up the Foundation Stone, and the three Hierarchies which are also described as Spirits of Strength, Spirits of Light, and Spirits of Soul. In this world of the Hierarchies, those forces are at work which Rudolf Steiner addresses as the World Love, World Imagination and World Thoughts. But the Foundation Stone has a double form, and its other part is formed out of human forces—out of Human Love, Human Imagination, and Human Thoughts. It is a concept almost impossible to grasp: this archetypal form, which comes to us as the Stone of Love, was moulded in the lap of the Hierarchies over thousands of years.

It is not so difficult to understand the First Hierarchy—Seraphim, Cherubim and Thrones—as the bearers of the reigning World Love. This is the Hierarchy which receives the plan of the world from spiritual heights, and uses its powers to realise it. The Creative Love of the Father God is shone into our evolving solar system by the Seraphim, as gleaming, world-creative Love. The Cherubim penetrate these mighty and still chaotic forces of Love with divine Wisdom, which harmonises them. The Thrones provide, through their power of sacrifice, the opportunity for a world to arise out of this Divine Love in which Man will be able to develop. In an exalted state of Grace, they bear the developing solar system. Love, therefore, which flows through all three choirs of the First Hierarchy, forms the actual substance of the Foundation Stone. It is the Hierarchy which creates beings which can pursue an independent existence and develop themselves further.

It is harder to grasp how the Second Hierarchy—Kyriotetes, Dynamis, Exusiai, (here also called Spirits of Light)—give the Foundation Stone its form and structure. World-Imaginations are here at work.

If one remembers what Rudolf Steiner has to say in his various works, including *Occult Science*, concerning the Second Hierarchy, then it becomes evident that this Hierarchy is always connected with Light. During the Sun-evolution, the Kyriotetes rayed forth their being as a gift of virtue. This gift of virtue was reflected back from the periphery, where the Archangels were at work, and appeared as light. It was still an inward light, not like the light of the Sun as it shines in the heavens today. In contrast, Old Saturn was shrouded in darkness.

A subsequent incarnation of our planet, the Old Moon, revealed the activity of the Dynamis. The astral body was born in the being of man, and it was filled with yearning for the spirit. The Dynamis stilled this yearning by carrying World-Imaginations to these astral bodies. A kind of consciousness appeared for the first time which could be compared with present-day dream consciousness, and which unfolded only in pictures. In the present Earth-evolution, the activity of the Exusiai is manifest from the Lemurian epoch on—and it is again an activity in the light. The Exusiai, working as Spirits of Form, summon the forms of living beings into appearance. Their activity is not to be found within the solid substance, the impenetrable part of earthly beings, but is manifest where the forms themselves appear out of the light. They work where the forms border, so to speak, on the spiritual world. Thus we have here, three times over, a Sun activity. The light produces forms, but forms which are pictures, or Imaginations. World-Imaginations are at work, and it is these which give the Foundation Stone its form.

The World-Thoughts, out of which the Foundation Stone shines towards us, are produced by the Third Hierarchy, the Archai, Archangels and Angels, which Rudolf Steiner also referred to as Spirits of Soul. At a deeper level, they are concerned with thinking, with World-Thinking. The Angels, as Rudolf Steiner often described, are connected with sense-perception. Their activity is to apprehend directly the appearances which arise around man. It is a thinking in concentrated form. Not for nothing is the eye, the sense-organ *par excellence*, a protuberance of the brain. When the gaze falls on an object in the external world, the entire content of the object is, in a deeper sense, actually grasped by the act of seeing, although spiritual Intuition is needed to perceive the nature of the process.

The Archangels are active where thinking itself takes place within the soul. Their concern is not the immediate content of the thoughts, but rather what the soul makes of the content as it works it over in thought. Finally, the Archai retain the thoughts firmly as memory pictures. Living in memory also calls upon thinking activity, but only makes use of unconscious or half-conscious forces to do so.

In these three aspects of thinking, the soul's forces of picturing, feeling and willing play distinct parts. In memories, the pictures rise up out of hidden realms of the will. They arise anew, awoken out of the etheric body through the activity of the Ego. The actual thinking process is an activity which flits back and forth between thinking and willing, in which at a deeper level, feeling also plays a significant part. The primary thought-activity is found in the thinking related to immediate sense-impressions, but the other two soul activities are needed to awaken it fully.

Through their World-Thoughts which have arisen in this way, the Third Hierarchy bestows upon the Foundation Stone its shining light.

The Foundation Stone Meditation is meant to lead us to recognise these creative activities of the Hierarchies, and then to offer to them our Love, our Imaginations, and our Thoughts, so that the Foundation Stone does not live separately from us as a creation of the Hierarchies only, but is re-formed again and again within us. In this way, it can become a Soul of World Man, creating a Body of World Man.

Man and Humanity

Rudolf Steiner often spoke of Christ as the "Representative of humanity". He also described Him as the "Ego of humanity". The notion of humanity is quite a recent one historically. In pre-Christian times, men generally spoke only of their own nation or tribe. The Greeks and Romans still referred to all people who did not belong to their own culture as barbarians. The Gods of the religions, too, were considered to belong to a particular nation or tribe. Jahve was the folk-spirit of the Jews. In Egypt, there was a whole series of Gods, who belonged to the various districts—even the towns had their particular divinities. The situation in ancient India was probably rather different; at that time men's gaze was so much directed towards the heavens that the earthly aspects of human life played only a minor part.

The situation only changed through the appearance of Christ on earth. Christ always speaks to the essential humanity in man, no matter to what people or tribe the individual belongs. This was why he provoked astonishment and anger among the orthodox Jews. In the history of humanity, this was something quite new.

Man is now to be regarded as a being who carries within him a germ of fundamental humanity, even though, at first, it is still completely hidden by the connections of family, nation and race. Until then, the human Ego had lived in the blood. But Christ spoke directly to this Ego, and led men to become aware that it is just the influence of the blood which holds them back from a true birth of the Ego. It is very curious to read, in the Epistles of St. Paul, the greetings which he sends to the members of the community to whom he is writing. Of the many he names, scarcely one is known to history. One was perhaps an aristocrat, another a slave, still another a craftsman. They probably belonged to quite different peoples or tribes. Through the Deed of Christ, an element had been introduced which was to grow steadily in importance as the evolution of man proceeded. The concept of a humanity, one may say, within which all men are children of God, was born for the first time.

The concept continued to exert its influence, and was deepened philosophically and scientifically in Humanism. But the task of shaping a true humanity could not be begun in a concrete way until the age of the Spiritual Soul. Gradually, all men have been linked externally together, at first through the voyages of discovery, by means of which all the races and peoples of the world became known, and then through the scientific discoveries which followed, which in due course made possible world-wide communications, intercourse, and trade. Terrible problems have arisen as a result, as the past decades and two world wars have shown. Today, humanity is externally a unity, in that there is no event on earth of any importance which does not directly or indirectly affect all men.

The task now, therefore, is for a true humanity in a deeper sense to emerge. This is not a matter of sentiment or "good will". It is not enough to wish or dream that "the time is now ripe". The mighty tasks of the future can only be performed if each individual learns to recognise within himself the forces which live spiritually in humanity as a whole, and which are to be realised on earth. This means the Christianising of the individual, who becomes a representative of true humanity in so far as he carries the Christ, the Ego of humanity, within him.

The whole of Anthroposophy, as it was given to man, is a preparation for this, for the understanding of the individual man in relation to the evolution of humanity as a whole. It may be remembered, for instance, that the chapter of *Occult Science* in which Rudolf Steiner describes the nine (or seven) members of man's being, is headed "The Nature of Humanity". In this connection, his accounts of national psychology should be mentioned, where he characterises the European peoples according to the different configuration of their soul-members. Characteristics of the individual are used there to epitomise the peoples. But the purpose of these descriptions of national psychology is not to enable the individual to recognise how his individuality is stamped by his nationality, but the opposite. The very fact that all peculiarities of different peoples are also found in the individual can help us to recognise that man was made for humanity.

Here too, the Foundation Stone Meditation offers us an opportunity to practise this. As already mentioned, the first parts of the three main sections are concerned with self-knowledge, while the second parts speak of humanity as it rests within the Divine Trinity and in the lap of the Hierarchies, only gradually achieving separate birth. In the first three sections the Ego is spoken of three times, in relation to how it learns to know itself within the human soul, in the threefold organism, and also in the Divine Trinity. Later, the meditation indicates how humanity as such is born or arises from out of the divine worlds. When, as it says, the Father Spirit of the Heights begets life in the Depths of Worlds, this Life is the life of evolving humanity. The First Hierarchy guides the divine creative powers out of the Heights into the Depths. What rings out from the Heights is echoed in the Depths, "speaking: Ex Deo nascimur", or "From God, Mankind has Being."

The working of the Christ within evolving humanity is described as blessing the Soul. His Will holds sway in the Rhythms of the Worlds, which take up all human hearts in the same rhythm. One may consider in meditation how a great wave of rhythms flows over the whole surface of the earth, which contains within it the rhythms of heart and lung of all individual human beings. Rudolf Steiner often spoke of the connection between the human heartbeat and the cosmic rhythms of the day, the span of life, and the Platonic Year. Although these rhythms of the blood differ in detail in individuals, they all originate in the great World-Rhythms. If one considers that the heart is the only organ which is really here on earth,* then one may truly say that this great wave which flows round the world, in which all hearts beat together,

* *Das Initiaten-Bewusstsein*, Dornach 1969. English translation, *True and False Paths of Spiritual Investigation*, London, 1969.

represents the first beginnings of a new earth. The earth is dying away all around us; but it is arising anew within the souls of men, and its first beginnings are to be found where the foundation for a new humanity is being formed, where the rhythms sound together.

The Will of the Christ works in the encircling Round —that is, within the totality of human beings who people the earth. The Second Hierarchy, which may also be regarded as the Hierarchy of the encircling Round, leads human development from East to West with its forces of light, while the formative forces from out of the West mould the fire forces of the East. Significant in this connection are Rudolf Steiner's words about the relationship between will and thought in East and West at the East-West Congress in Vienna: "The Will of the West must strengthen the thought of the East and the thought of the West redeem the will of the East".

In the processes indicated here, death is overcome by the new life flowing into humanity through Christ. "In Christo morimur"; "In Christ, Death becomes Life".

It is clear that through the activity of the Holy Spirit, humanity as such will be brought to an awakening. The first revelation of the working of the Holy Spirit was the Whitsun Event: The spirit began to speak in different ways out of individual men; but its language could be understood by men of all peoples and tribes. The Whitsun Event points to a far future, in which the human being will be filled individually with the Spirit, will have become an Ego in a higher sense; but this Spirit, and this Ego, will reveal themselves as living simultaneously in humanity as a whole.

Man rises up to the Third Hierarchy, and in his thinking enters into the sphere of the Angels. In his personal relations with his fellow men, he enters the sphere of the Archangels. And in his relation to the nature of Time, he enters the sphere of the Archai. The Foundation Stone Meditation addresses the Third Hierarchy with the words: "Spirits of Soul: Let this be prayed in the Depths and from the Heights be answered". And the reply is: "Per Spiritum Sanctum reviviscimus". "In the Spirit's Universal Thoughts the Soul awakens". One can also say: "the soul awakens within the Spirit of Humanity".

It has already been mentioned that the Foundation Stone was guided down from spiritual heights by Rudolf Steiner, and received into the souls of all those present, into hearts which "through their harmonious cooperation, their goodwill imbued with love, carry the Anthroposophical purpose through the world together". With this, the Foundation Stone was laid into the substance out of which a new earth is to be born. The meaning of this may perhaps be grasped more deeply if one remembers that Rudolf Steiner, on the occasion of the laying of the first Foundation Stone in 1913, gave the first beginnings of the Fifth Gospel. At the time he indicated that this was connected with the forces which work from the Old Moon to Jupiter. In the laying of the Foundation Stone of 1923, it was then possible to experience the future Jupiter existence as a condition in which a humanity, filled with the Spirit, will be formed from the Spirit-Selves of individual human beings.

Rudolf Steiner's Departure

The General Anthroposophical Society, which received its form through the Christmas Meeting, had an organic structure. It has already been mentioned that the national societies—after they had become clear about their tasks—had banded together as the General Anthroposophical Society, in order to realise, through this merging, the wide human aims of the movement. Through joining together, their own tasks were deepened in relation to the needs of humanity at large. In a sense, therefore, the children had appeared before the mother was born. But when the mother appeared, the children could recognise their own nature in her being.

During the Foundation Meeting at Christmas 1923, Rudolf Steiner proposed the formation of the *Vorstand* in which he was to have the role of *Vorsitzender* (President). The meeting agreed with great enthusiasm.

This *Vorstand* was conceived as a small group existing within the Society whose task was leadership and initiative. "To live Anthroposophy and put it into practice" was to be the Vorstand's prime task. The officials of the different national societies had, so to speak, a standing invitation which enabled them, when in Dornach, to consider themselves as members of the Vorstand not only as advisers, but, as Rudolf Steiner expressed it, as members with equal rights. Every arrangement for the future was made on the basis of "we". Rudolf Steiner always spoke of the Vorstand as a unity: "The Vorstand will" or "the Vorstand has". In the Statutes, the national societies were not mentioned as such. Only "Groups formed locally or for particular purposes" are referred to. The word "we" is used throughout. It was expected that the members everywhere would experience themselves as groups in new social forms. "The cultivation of the soul on the basis of knowledge of the spiritual world" was the general theme. One may also say that through the Christmas meeting a general summons went out to each individual to experience himself *within the Society*, and to assist consciously in carrying this community. The Foundation Stone Meditation provided the path to this experience.

For the Free High School, other Statutes are involved. To begin with, Rudolf Steiner took over the leadership of this High School, as he himself said. In this role, his task was to work as a spiritual teacher in all aspects of the anthroposophical life. The First Class was established by him and also brought to a provisional conclusion. A beginning was made in the Medical Section towards putting the different Sections on an esoteric basis. The Sections were linked as such to the First Class, and only members of the Class could belong to their respective Sections.

It is clear that Rudolf Steiner made a tremendous sacrifice in linking himself with the Society in so intimate a way. That he did so was a spiritual event of the deepest significance, not only for his own destiny but for that of all members. When a spiritual teacher links himself to his pupils, it means that he takes upon himself their destinies as well. From the Foundation Meeting on, there existed not only the personal relationship of teacher to pupil, which had held in very many cases previously, but the Teacher, as first *Vorsitzender* of the Society, also embraced all the members into his own Karma. This esoteric element, as Rudolf Steiner said, was now to imbue the whole Movement. As a result, everything which the members neglected to do or failed to comprehend in this respect would from then on represent a direct obstacle in Rudolf Steiner's own path. He wished to bring the members to recognise themselves and each other against the background of the historical stream to which they belonged. In this way, truly fraternal feeling could arise and be cultivated even between strongly contrasting personalities. Each member was gradually to come to know the spiritual streams which, within the various Mysteries, had prepared over thousands of years for the Mystery of Golgotha and its subsequent effects. In particular, Rudolf Steiner described, in mighty spiritual pictures, the events which had taken place in the spiritual world since the twelfth century: the spiritual council of the leading representatives of these streams, the Michael School, and the Cosmic Cult. It was made clear that very, very many of those who found their way into the Anthroposophical Movement on earth had taken part in these events previously.

When one now looks back after 33 years on this indescribably exalted revelation, one can see what a responsibility the members took upon themselves, simply through listening to these revelations apart from anything else. And when one then considers that the manner in which they reacted could be directly helpful or harmful to Rudolf Steiner, it is not surpising that after a time Rudolf Steiner fell ill. He himself indicated that his illness was not due to overwork, giving too many lectures or such like, but rather to endless conversations. It became clear that the members did not respond inwardly to his impulses, but rather loaded him with their personal problems. During September 1924, the last month of his active work among the members, ten to fifteen such conversations took place each day, in between the four to five lectures which he held daily.

We have seen how the first Goetheanum went up in flames. Rudolf Steiner had brought down from exalted spiritual realms the formative forces for this Goetheanum Being, built as it was on the frontier of the physical and the etheric worlds. One may also say that the forces of his own etheric sheath were built into it. When the building met its fiery death, not only Rudolf Steiner's work but his own life-forces were affected. One could feel that from then on he had constantly to take new life-forces into himself from the cosmic spaces. During his lectures, he could live directly in the spirit and renew himself from the spirit; but when he had to concern himself on the physical plane with all kinds of external problems, or with people and all their complications, his organism was worn down. His body was like a fragile sheath after the fire. When this sheath lit up, illumined by the spirit, one experienced the mighty forces of his spiritual being.

During his illness, he could no longer speak to the members as before; nevertheless, he wrote every day the

Letters which contained both the last and the highest of what he still had to say. His death, as has already been mentioned in the introduction to this book, was taken up into the great Mystery which an attempt has here been made to describe; it appeared as the fourth phase of this Mystery. The laying of the first Foundation Stone made the Stone visible in physical, mineral, form as a double pentagonal dodecahedron. As the Goetheanum grew, its forms and colours became a path of training for Imaginative consciousness. Although it was brought down from the highest spiritual worlds and reborn as Inspiration in Rudolf Steiner's soul, it displayed its nature on earth in image form, only to be fully apprehended by Imaginative consciousness. The Foundation Stone which was laid in the hearts of men in 1923, was the transformed Goetheanum itself. For the images carried up by the flames and transformed in the fire, came resounding back from the spiritual heights in the words of the Foundation Stone, to be experienced in *Inspiration.*

Just as the Goetheanum building rose up on the first Foundation Stone, so the General Anthroposophical Society was to grow up from the second Foundation Stone as a society in which the human soul could be at home. Rudolf Steiner's departure into the spiritual world was for us a shattering sign that the individual was not yet in a position to make the necessary sacrifices to form this new spiritual community. This departure, therefore, could become for us the task of developing *Intuitive* consciousness.

In Imagination, the soul rises up to the pictures which reveal themselves spiritually; but these pictures, although they have a spiritual origin, still have a subjective colouring. The Imaginations must be banished once more from the soul, they must be removed by auto-suggestion, as Rudolf Steiner also expressed it. The aim is to remain awake with an empty consciousness, so that the spiritual world may allow its Inspirations to stream in. But to achieve Intuition, all egotism must have been overcome, so that the pure will may become a vessel for the Will of the Spirit. In Intuition, Rudolf Steiner also once said, one gives oneself to the Gods as food, one allows oneself to be consumed by them.

With these inadequate words the fourth phase of the Mystery which is connected with the Foundation Stone may perhaps be expressed. Following Rudolf Steiner's death, the central task can only be the spiritual awakening of the Ego in each individual, and the further treading of anthroposophical paths in free community. In this sense it will be possible to speak of a continuation of the impulse of the Christmas Meeting.

The Pentagram and the Sun of Christ

We know that in mantric verses, as Rudolf Steiner always emphasised, each word has a quite precise meaning. Thus one may ask what is expressed in these five sayings about Light. It is clear that five different qualities of Light are addressed. What can it mean, for instance, that the "Spirit-Light of the World" enters the stream of Earthly Being? It is the Light of the Holy Spirit that is being referred to here, the Light of the Divine Sophia. It may be remembered that according to Rudolf Steiner, the true name of the mother of the Nathan Jesus was Sophia. This Sophia entered the stream of earthly being.

The verse goes on to say that darkness of night had held its sway, and day-radiant Light poured into the souls of men. Here again, a particular quality of Light is expressed: day-radiant Light that is to work in human souls; a Light, in other words, that awakens a new consciousness; the Light of Consciousness, that streams out from Michael.

Next there is named that Light which gives warmth to simple shepherds' hearts—and immediately following, that Light which enlightens the wise heads of Kings.

We can recognise these two qualities of Light from the descriptions in the Gospels, which were explained by Rudolf Steiner. The first Light—that which was seen by the shepherds in the fields—is a heavenly Light in which the Buddha Being shines, the Nirmanakaya of the Buddha. The second Light, that enlightens the wise heads of the Kings, is the Light of Zarathustra, the Zarathustra Star. We know that the three Kings from the West were spiritual pupils of Zarathustra, and that it was Zarathustra who led them to Palestine.

The fifth Light is the "Light Divine". This Light has a quite special quality which can only be expressed by calling it "divine"—for it is the Light of the original Soul of Humanity, the Nathan Being itself, the Light-Soul, so to speak, which was preserved in the spiritual world untouched by the Fall. It was kept thus, in the Mother-Lodge of humanity, so that it might incarnate at the turning-point of time, and become the bearer of the Christ-Being.

When these five qualities of Light have been named, the totality appears, the Sun of Christ, which carries all five within it.

Rudolf Steiner made it possible for us to understand this all-embracing Christ Being. His own path took him from the world of scientific and philosophical thinking to an ever deeper inwardness—until, as he expressed it, he stood before the Mystery of Golgotha "in a most inward, most solemn festival of knowledge". His relation to the Christ Being is not a matter of faith or religious confession, but is a most fundamental personal experience. For this reason he could recognise that which stands in the Gospels as an open secret, the fact of the two Jesus children. Through his own spiritual researches he came to recognise the great significance of the Zarathustra Being, who incarnated in the Solomon

Jesus child, and the deed of the Buddha in connection with the birth of the Nathan Jesus. In the same way he could clearly recognise the Being of Michael, whom he described as the Countenance of Christ. He repeatedly described the comprehensive significance of the Divine Sophia.

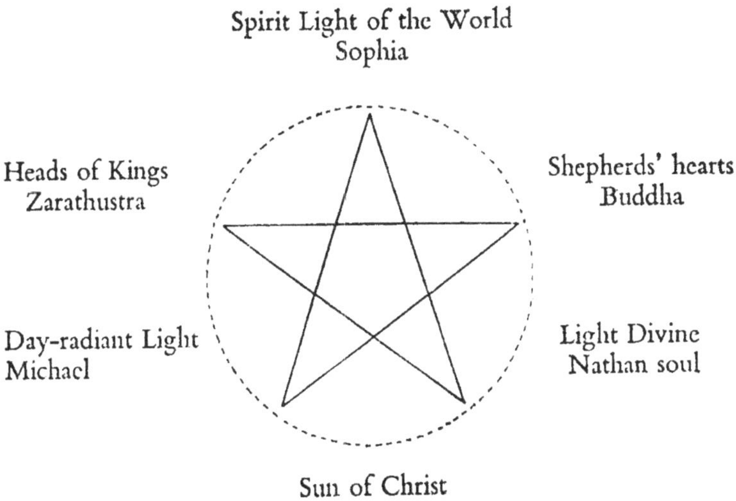

Thus through Rudolf Steiner, all that he had gathered from the periphery of the world into his innermost being could shine out again over all fields of knowledge and over artistic and social activity. He taught us to understand that the Christ Being is an all-penetrating, all-embracing reality, whose infinite greatness will only be comprehended in future times.

The Foundation Stone meditation also includes the three Rosicrucian sayings. They have not yet been mentioned in this connection. Perhaps the following may be indicated here: In the *Fama Fraternitas* it is related that a hundred years after the death of Christian

Rosenkreutz, his grave was found, and when it was opened, his body lay there unblemished. Christian Rosenkreutz held in his hand a small book with a short description of his life and teaching. The title of the final chapter was: "Granum pectori Jesu insitum"—"a seed in the heart of Jesus". The three sayings about birth, death and resurrection are in a certain sense the most intimate Christian secret. One may say of Christian Rosenkreutz that he took the opposite path to Rudolf Steiner: it led from within outwards; from out of his innermost being he strove outwards to knowledge of the world, in order to make this world-knowledge inward again. That is the Rosicrucian path. Both Rudolf Steiner and Christian Rosenkreutz lead the Sun of Christ to us, but their ways of working—leading from without, inwards and then out again, or from within, outwards and then back to inwardness—constantly interpenetrate each other, like delicate red and blue hues, producing through this mingling the peach-blossom colour of the etheric, in which the Sun of Christ lights up for us.

The carving of the Representative of Humanity holding the balance between Lucifer and Ahriman, was to have been placed beneath the small dome of the first Goetheanum so that everyone entering the building by the West door could have felt that Christ was coming towards him.

The fourth main section of the Foundation Stone Meditation, "At the turning point of Time", contains a metamorphosis of this statue. It speaks of the Spirit-Light of the World, Divine Light, Sun of Christ. Ahriman and Lucifer are not mentioned; they are already overcome. The "Light that gives warmth to simple Shepherds' hearts" is not the Luciferic light, that causes the human heart-forces to climb like a devouring flame above the head. Neither is the Light which "enlightens the Wise heads of Kings" the cold light of intelligence in which Ahriman lies as though caught in a net.

Light is mentioned five times in this part of the Meditation; Spirit-Light of the World; Day-radiant Light; Light that warms; Light that enlightens, and Light Divine. One can regard these five words of Light as a five-pointed star, a kind of Light-Pentagram, which has entered the "stream of Earthly Being" from Divine Heights.

But the statue contains a further secret, as Rudolf Steiner said in a lecture*. This carving is, fundamentally, only a veil covering an invisible sculpture. The invisible statue is the new Isis, the Isis of a new age. It is not that the association of the Representative of Humanity with Lucifer and Ahriman "means" the Isis, as Rudolf Steiner emphasised. The Beings who make up the group are what they appear to be. But behind them, nevertheless, is a true Being, the new Isis, the sleeping Isis. He said that on this real and deeper statue a script could be seen as clearly as in the script on the earlier, veiled statue of Isis, which read: "I am the All, I am the Past, the Present and the Future. No mortal has yet lifted my veil". Today, the script reads: "I am Man, I am the Past, the Present and the Future. Every mortal shall lift my veil".

The lecture in which this is contained relates the new Isis and Osiris myth, as Rudolf Steiner called it. It cannot be summarised here, since the way in which he spoke, using imaginative images and indications, can only be expressed in his own words. But enough may be said here to enable the connection between the script above the Isis picture, and its metamorphosis in the Foundation Stone Meditation to be understood.

Rudolf Steiner says that in the land of Philisterium, on a lonely hill, there stood a building which revealed, in Goethe's sense, an 'open secret'. Everybody could go there, but most saw nothing. The centre-piece of the building was a statue. A visitor came and approached the

*Lecture in the cycle *Alte Mythen und Ihre Bedeutung*. given on 6th January 1918. Dornach 1937. English translation, typescript R-L11 available to members of the Anthroposophical Society.

sleeping form of the new Isis many times. The new Isis bore a son, and believed that the visitor, whom she loved and considered to be her special benefactor, was the father of this offspring. The visitor, too, considered himself—wrongly—to be the father. He was the new Typhon, who believed that he could increase his strength in a special way if he took possession of the new Isis. The latter took her son through many parts of the world, and through the power of the world itself he fell into fourteen pieces. The new Typhon collected up the fourteen pieces and made out of them, "with all the knowledge derived from the profundities of science", a Being governed only by mechanical, machine-like laws. This Being, which had an appearance of life, could multiply itself again by fourteen. Typhon gave to each a reflection of his own being, so that "each of the fourteen sons of the new Isis acquired a face which resembled that of Typhon". Isis regarded these wonders with dawning understanding. She was conscious that it was she herself who had brought it all about. "But a day arrived when she saw the true nature of this Being with the help of a number of Elemental Nature Spirits". At this moment she perceived clairvoyantly that she still possessed her cow horns from Ancient Egypt—but the power of her clairvoyance was produced by Typhon himself (some say by Mercury), and he placed a crown on the part of her head where the old Isis once wore the golden crown which Horus tore from her. But the new crown was made of plain paper "covered with writings on all kinds of deep scientific knowledge". "One day, through the power of her clairvoyance, she realised the deep meaning of that which is described in the Gospel of St. John as the Logos, and which could be realised by her age. She understood the Johannine meaning of the Mystery of Golgotha. Through this power, the might of the cow horns took hold of the paper crown and transformed it into a real golden crown of true wisdom".

Through patient meditative practice, this new Osiris myth can be understood as a great revelation concerning the working of the Holy Spirit.

The Being of Osiris and Isis, as it lived in the ancient Mysteries, points to the earliest period of the earth's evolution. This pair of Gods were originally experienced as working from the world of the fixed stars, from the direction which Sirius and Orion stood in the sky. It is possible that the old Egyptian initiates regarded this region of the heavens as a kind of gate through which the Divine Spirit could send its forces into our solar system. Later, Isis and Osiris were connected with Sun and Moon. Later still, at the time when wisdom concerning the Elements was pre-eminent, the path of Initiation led through these Elements into the realm of the Music of the Spheres. Here, Isis appeared as a World Mother, giving birth to Osiris as Logos. There sounded forth the cosmic Word.*

Since the year 1322 B.C., this birth of Osiris could no longer be experienced. The Imaginative consciousness which men had attained up till then was lost. The time came when men perceived the external world through

* *Die Mysterien des Morgenlandes und des Christentums*, Dornach 1960. English translation, *Mysteries of the East and of Christianity*, London, 1972.

their sense-organs. The Osiris-Isis myth, which imbued the whole ancient Egyptian culture, described this loss of Imaginative consciousness. It expressed the whole tragedy of the Initiates, who experienced the death of the Sun God. The myth appears in which Osiris is a King and Teacher, who was killed by Typhon and sealed in a coffin. This was carried away by the Nile, and was found again by Isis at Biblos in Phoenicia. From this land came the written symbols, the dead letters, which were to replace the language of Imagination. Since this time, according to the myth, Osiris is the judge of the dead in the underworld. Nevertheless, he fertilises Isis with a ray of light, as a result of which the Horus child is born. When Horus grows up, and learns that Isis allowed Typhon to go free, he tears off her crown of stars in a rage and replaces it with the cow horns.

In his new Osiris-Isis myth, Steiner's aim is to show that today, in this age of the Spiritual Soul, in which the Egyptian cultural epoch is being recapitulated, Imaginative consciousness must be attained again. This involves passing through a series of illusions which have taken hold of the souls of men in the age of scientific "profundities". Even the sleeping Isis, the Being of true Humanity which is sleeping within man, is affected by these illusions. But the power of the Mystery of Golgotha works through the unconscious forces of the soul and provides an opportunity to understand the words in the Gospel of St. John: "In the Beginning was the Word." "The power of the Word, the Power of the Logos, must be taken hold of again". In an age which lives in abstractions, and in which concepts only exist as dead thoughts, man will only make progress when he learns to experience anew the creative power of the Word within him.

The script on the Statue, in which the new Isis leads a veiled existence, reads: "I am Man, I am the past, the present and the future. Every mortal shall lift my veil". This clearly says that Isis is Man—but Man reborn out of the Spirit in the sense in which Christ spoke to Nicodemus of the reborn man.

The Foundation Stone Meditation points the way directly to this rebirth out of the Spirit. "I am Man". Who man is, is defined by the three sections of the Meditation which begin "Soul of Man"—the Soul of Man which lives in the three parts of the threefold organism. Then follows: "I am the past, the present and the future". In the Foundation Stone Meditation there follow the three exercises through which the Ego can experience itself in relation to the past, present and future. "Every mortal shall lift my veil". It is now possible for man to recognise his Divine origin, "for . . . ". Then follow the three great cosmic sections of the Meditation, which reveal the Being of Man as it originates with the Trinity and is then given the possibility of realising itself on earth through the Hierarchies.

Thus may the true Man be born in us as Anthroposophia, as a Being which is an individual bearer of the all-pervading Spirit.

In the Foundation Stone Meditation it is said that the Elemental Beings can already hear the mighty messages of the Hierarchies, and that they hear the Divine Light and the Sun of Christ sounding. The spiritual garment which will clothe the true form of man in the future will be woven out of the etheric, the world of the Elements. The new myth says that the Elemental Beings give back to Isis her son in his true form.

This indication of the picture of future man concludes this book. The way in which Man will one day appear as bearer of the World-Ego can only be dimly apprehended today. Nevertheless, further development of the forces of the soul will permit us, in due course, to behold the perfected figure of Man with the eye of the Spirit.

Menschenseele!
Du lebest in den Gliedern,
Die dich durch die Raumeswelt
In das Geistesmeereswesen tragen:
Übe *Geist-Erinnern*
In Seelentiefen,
Wo in waltendem
Weltenschöpfer-Sein
Das eigne Ich
Im Gottes-Ich
Erweset;
Und du wirst wahrhaft *leben*
Im Menschen-Welten-Wesen

Denn es waltet der Vater-Geist der Höhen
In den Weltentiefen Sein-erzeugend.
Seraphim, Cherubim, Throne,
Lasset aus den Höhen erklingen,
Was in den Tiefen das Echo findet;
Dieses spricht:
Ex Deo nascimur.
Das hören die Elementargeister
Im Osten, Westen, Norden, Süden:
Menschen mögen es hören.

Menschenseele!
Du lebest in dem Herzens-Lungen-Schlage,
Der dich durch den Zeitenrhythmus
Ins eigne Seelenwesensfühlen leitet:
Übe *Geist-Besinnen*
Im Seelengleichgewichte,

Wo die wogenden
Welten-Werde-Taten
Das eigne Ich
Dem Welten-Ich
Vereinen;
Und du wirst wahrhaft *fühlen*
Im Menschen-Seelen-Wirken.

Denn es waltet der Christus-Wille im Umkreis
In den Weltenrythmen Seelen-begnadend.
Kyriotetes, Dynamis, Exusiai,
Lasset vom Osten befeuern,
Was durch den Westen sich gestaltet;
Dieses spricht:
In Christo morimur.
Das hören die Elementargeister
Im Osten, Westen, Norden, Süden:
Menschen mögen es hören.

Menschenseele!
Du lebest im ruhenden Haupte,
Das dir aus Ewigkeitsgründen
Die Weltgedanken erschliesset:
Übe *Geist-Erschauen*,
In Gedanken-Ruhe,
Wo die ew'gen Götterziele
Welten-Wesens-Licht
Dem eignen Ich
Zu freiem Wollen
Schenken;
Und du wirst wahrhaft *denken*
In Menschen-Geistes-Gründen.

Denn es walten des Geistes Weltgedanken
Im Weltenwesen Licht-erflehend.
Archai, Archangeloi, Angeloi,
O lasset aus den Tiefen erbitten,
Was in den Höhen erhöret wird;
Dieses spricht:
Per spiritum sanctum reviviscimus.
Das hören die Elementargeister
Im Osten, Westen, Norden, Süden:
Menschen mögen es hören.

In der Zeiten Wende
Trat das Welten-Geistes-Licht
In den Irdischen Wesensstrom;
Nacht-Dunkel
Hatte ausgewaltet,
Taghelles Licht
Erstrahlte in Menschenseelen;
Licht,
Das erwärmet
Die armen Hirtenherzen;
Licht,
Das erleuchtet
Die weisen Königshäupter.

Göttliches Licht,
Christus-Sonne,
Erwärme
Unsere Herzen;
Erleuchte
Unsere Häupter;

Dass gut werde,
Was wir
Aus Herzen gründen,
Aus Häuptern
Zielvoll führen wollen.

(Text of the Foundation Stone Meditation as spoken by Rudolf Steiner on 1st January 1924. From *Die Grundsteinlegung*, Verlag der Rudolf Steiner Nachlassverwaltung, Dornach, 1955).

Soul of Man!
Thou livest in the Limbs
Which bear thee through the world of Space
Into the ocean-being of the Spirit.
Practise *Spirit-recollection*
In depths of soul,
Where in the wielding
World-Creator-Life
Thine own I comes to being
Within the I of God.
Then in the All-World-Being of Man
Thou wilt truly *live*.

For the Father-Spirit of the Heights holds sway
In Depths of Worlds begetting Life.
Seraphim, Cherubim, Thrones!
Let there ring out from the Heights
What in the Depths is echoed,
Speaking:
Ex Deo nascimur.

The Elemental Spirits hear it
In East and West and North and South:
May human beings hear it!

Soul of Man!
Thou livest in the beat of Heart and Lung
Which leads thee through the rhythmic tides of Time
Into the feeling of thine own Soul-being.
Practise *Spirit-mindfulness*
In balance of the soul,
Where the surging
Deeds of the World's Becoming
Do thine own I unite
Unto the I of the World.
Then 'mid the weaving of the Soul of Man
Thou wilt truly *feel*.

For the Christ-Will in the encircling Round holds
sway
In the Rhythms of the Worlds, blessing the Soul.
Kyriotetes, Dynamis, Exusiai!
Let there be fired from the East
What through the West is formèd,
Speaking:
In Christo morimur.
The Elemental Spirits hear it
In East and West and North and South.
May human beings hear it!

Soul of Man!
Thou livest in the resting Head

Which from the ground of the Eternal
Opens to thee the Thoughts of Worlds.
Practise *Spirit-vision*
In quietness of Thought,
Where the eternal aims of Gods
World-Being's Light
On thine own I bestow
For thy free Willing.
Then from the ground of the Spirit in Man
Thou wilt truly *think*.

For the Spirit's Universal Thoughts hold sway
In the Being of all Worlds, craving for Light.
Archai, Archangeloi, Angeloi!
Let there be prayed in the Depths
What from the Heights is answered,
Speaking:
Per spiritum sanctum reviviscimus.
The Elemental Spirits hear it
In East and West and North and South:
May human beings hear it!

At the turning-point of Time
The Spirit-Light of the World
Entered the stream of Earthly Being.
Darkness of Night
Had held its sway;
Day-radiant Light
Poured into the souls of men:
Light that gives warmth
To simple Shepherds' Hearts,

Light that enlightens
The wise Heads of Kings.

O Light Divine,
O Sun of Christ!
Warm Thou our Hearts,
Enlighten Thou our Heads,
That good may become
What from our Hearts we would found,
And from our Heads direct
With single purpose.

(Translation from *The Foundation Stone*, London, 1957

Emanuel Zeylmans

Willem Zeylmans van Emmichoven

An Inspiration for Anthroposophy, A Biography

Born in Holland in 1893, Zeylmans van Emmichoven was one of the original pioneers of anthroposophy, the science of spirit established by Rudolf Steiner. As General Secretary of the Anthroposophical Society in the Netherlands, he worked closely with Steiner. A medical doctor and founder of the Rudolf Steiner Clinic in Scheveningen, he also conducted important research into the influence of colours, the psychology of peoples and nations, and individual human psychology.

Emanuel Zeylmans' biography of his father draws on some beautifully written and moving autobiographical extracts as well as numerous other first-hand source materials. He traces Zeylmans' remarkable life from his upbringing in Holland and his first contact with Rudolf Steiner to his later attendance at the momentous Christmas Foundation Meeting and his many travels around the world to further anthroposophy. He examines the spiritual conflicts in which Zeylmans became embroiled, his life during the war years, and his innovative work in many fields. The author also catalogues Zeylmans' written works, and gives a full chronology of his life.

Willem Zeylmans van Emmichoven is a compelling documentation of a leading figure connected with Rudolf Steiner. It brings to life the context of his biography—an exciting and yet difficult time in the development of new spiritual ideas—and the vibrant individuals around him. Zeylmans is portrayed as a warm, dynamic and fascinating individual, with enormous interest in people from widely differing cultures and backgrounds. A real 'world citizen', he recognized that every nation has its own particular task and importance.

312pp (8 b/w plates + illus.); 24 × 16 cm; hardback; £20; ISBN: 1 902636 35 X